●●●●●●●●●●●●●●●●●●●●●●●●

LAUGHTER IN THE ROAR

●●●●●●●●●●●●●●●●●●●●●●●●

● ● ● ● ● ● ● ● ● ● ● ● ● ●

LAUGHTER IN
THE ROAR

● ● ● ● ● ● ● ● ● ● ● ● ● ●

Reminiscences of

Variety and Pantomime

by

Brian O'Gorman

1998

LAUGHTER IN THE ROAR
© Brian O'Gorman, 1998
Published by Brian O'Gorman,
1, Rivermead Close, Addlestone, Weybridge, Surrey KT15 2DR

Printed by The Badger Press, Westbury, Wiltshire

ISBN 0 9534078 0 2

Photographs and illustrations

Dave and Joe O'Gorman, 1949

OVERTURE

"He used to work on the Halls you know." Certainly he did. But how did he get started? What made him want to?

Sir Laurence Olivier in response to the same query said, "Surely you know that all actors are saying, 'Look at me! Look at me!' And this is fundamental, but more so for the Variety Artiste, because, while the straight actor is playing a part, creating a character and hoping to lose himself in it, the entertainer is projecting his own personality. He offers himself for approval. And it has to be instant, immediately warranted, not like the applause at the end of a play, which follows the carefully constructed denouement."

Consider some catch phrases: "Mum! Mum! They're laughing at me again;" "Can you hear me Mother?" "You Lucky People;" "Miller's the name lady; There'll never be another;" "Mind my bike!" "I've only got five minutes." The appeal for sympathetic awareness could hardly be put more plainly. The crashing emotional burden of failure, or the fear of it has been the subject of many plays, books and films.

But the avid young idea will not be deterred. Amateur productions, church socials, children's parties; somewhat up the scale, Masonics, club dinners, all providing experience and some pocket money perhaps. And the chance to be noticed and perhaps written up.

At the Music Hall's heyday there were "Extra Turns" and "Trial Turns." One of the group associated with the Brixton Set, including Charlie Chaplin, Connie Emerald (Ida Lupino's mother), Hetty and Edie Kelly, was a stage struck lad called Tom Payne, a likeable fellow with more hope than talent. He determined to do a Trial Turn at the Montpelier, in the G. H. Elliott style - blacked up. His friends were anxious to dissuade him and volunteered to make him up, but with grease and not the usual burnt cork.

When Tom got on the stage, with the heat, his natural anxiety and the "work" he put in his song, the sweat and grease ran in rivulets down his face, producing a hilarious effect quite different from the one intended and he left the stage in confusion. It was a hard lesson to be taught, but in any event it cured him of his ambitions.

But success as Trial Turn might bring an offer of a week at ..... at a salary of £x; twice as large as present earnings. But the date is out of London. No chance of doing a day job as well. And this is decision time. No going back after this. Our hero has got to choose; to be a "Pro" or settle for a life of unremarkable work and even modest prosperity. His friends will be encouraging, "You have such talent." "Better than this boring old routine." "Look at Charlie Thompson. He's earning £100 a week." And he will choose, to get his band parts and his props together and go to Hetton-le-Hole, for it is his destiny; he must do it.

And then the real life begins.

On the Wednesday he phones the Agent who has booked him. "No nothing for next week, but drop in while you are in town and we will fix something up." But at least he has an Agent, who is working for him. And, after three weeks, a rush phone call. "I can fix you at the Hippo, Marshland. Only £y. But as it's London you will save expenses, living at home." (£y is £1 less than his job had been paying.)

So he accepts because needs must and Marshland is a place where bookers for the circuits are known to go. Incredibly one does and comes round to see him. "You have got something to offer. But your first song is no good. Tempo too slow. And that patter about the gasworks. Better cut it out. Slows everything up. (He had thought this, based on audience response, the best bit of his act.) And you must get better clothes than that. First impressions are so important. Tell you what, let me know when you're working in town again and I'll come and have a look."

And with incredible perseverance, crust and charm, in equal measure and a bit of bloody-mindedness from time to time, a good deal of luck, a sympathetic audience or two (for no apparent reason) he begins to make his mark. (Oh! And he has two new suits. And the bill for them.) He joins the V.A.F., gets a Railway Concession card and a list of approved lodgings. His date book is pencilled in for some while ahead. His salary has increased five times.

And he begins to get worried about his income tax.

Alec Navarre featured on the cover of The Perfomer, dated 15th April 1937

LAUGHTER IN THE ROAR

My collection of writings and reminiscences has been put together for several reasons: to preserve what is in danger of being forgotten, or was not known before; to convey the remembered atmosphere of the Variety theatres; to recall turns and Pantomimes; to capture something of styles of working and presentation; to record impressions received by one who was able to observe closely, from out front, or from the side of the stage, and to spark discussion among those who know, or do not know, of the captivating charms of the most direct and atmospheric of the Theatre's forms.

These recollections are, not unnaturally, based on my family's intimate participation in the Business for a period of 75 years.

But this is, so to speak, a hanger to put one's coat on. At one time there were 6,000 members of the V.A.F. It is by association that recognition is given to some of them; famous and not so famous.

Nor is this all. The performers in what are called "Irregular Forms" were, in general, not anxious to intellectualise their work. To be entertaining was the aim: the surest way to secure a long contract or a return date. What was "Box Office" was always sought and cherished. The intellectual sphere has been, notoriously, poison.

The Variety Artiste aimed to please, to provide amusement for those seeking a few hours' diversion, to enter a theatre and come out smiling, laughing, or even singing a song they had just heard. To be known as a popular favourite conveyed both senses of the term "popular." It was a title earned by many unsung, even unremembered, performers who deserve some appreciation of their work.

Also to be emphasised is that these forms of entertainment were, in no sense, a "Lark" for those involved. The skill involved in "doing your act" was truly that art which conceals art. There were conventions about getting on, registering and getting off. Learning the skills and polishing one's offering took many years of refinement. An instantaneous success was inclined to be a mill stone. Furthermore, the search for material to work up into an acceptable professional act and maintain that standard was a pressing concern.

"There's No Business like Show Business ...... the heartaches, the back aches, the flops."

My endeavour is to show something of the participants and what they were like. What did it feel like to get on, make an entrance, be effective, leave at the right time, register and get off? The directness of the activity is a major part of its appeal. I hope there is something of it to be found in these pages. I hope each reader finds some of the pleasure in the book that I have experienced in writing it.

"There's my music ......"

- ooOoo -

To avoid confusion and to clarify what may be misunderstood owing to a similarity of names, the following biographical details may be helpful.

Joe O'Gorman Snr. Born 1863 – died 1937

Celebrated as Tennyson and O'Gorman (The Two Irish Gentlemen) and, from 1901 as "The Irish Raconteur" in Variety, Revue and Pantomime.

First Chairman of the Variety Artistes Federation (Number One) and active in the Water Rats from its earliest days (twice King Rat) and in the foundation of Brinsworth. He represented the V.A.F. in the Strike and Arbitrations of 1907.

His sons, Dave and Joe O'Gorman Jnr., earlier, until 1932, billed as the O'Gorman Brothers, working from 1904 until 1956, also in Variety, Revue, Pantomime and Cabaret. Dave O'Gorman also King Rat (1956) and Chairman of the V.A.F.

Dave O'Gorman died in 1964 and Joe O'Gorman in 1974. Command Performers in 1938 and 1946, though not featured turns. By marriage the family was related to an extensive network in the Entertainment World.

Dave and Joe O'Gorman starting out

THE ENTERTAINERS ENTERTAINED

Because the Variety Theatre was devoted to popular entertainment and the haunt of Funny Men, it has come to be considered, by so many, "stagey," "theatrical," light-hearted and, therefore, impossible to take seriously, as if the protagonists could not possibly have had a serious or conscious thought in their heads. It is easy to debunk, guy, parody or belittle the popular entertainer as dealing in trivialities and, therefore, being of no account in themselves. Nothing could be further from the truth.

Variety performers were, of necessity, hard-working and thoughtful people. And some consideration of their leisure activities can help to focus on these aspects of the background to their performing lives.

That some were feckless, improvident and haphazardly disorganised, cannot be denied. But in these respects no more or less than the ordinary citizen.

But the people in this section, a very small cross-section, but a representative one, showed themselves serious-minded, thoughtful, sober and be able to be involved in and master activities which require concentration and which, at the same time, provided them with relaxation and fun away from the theatre. But positive virtues are not so surprising perhaps, because personality, ingenuity, style, enthusiasm, gusto are the precise essentials for selling one's act, creating an impression and relating to an audience. Their playthings were often exactly those of others who possessed a more than ample sufficiency of the world's goods.

The activities which performers undertook were perforce those which could be dropped and picked up again, either at home or during times away. Heavy "Do -it-yourself" does not fall easily into this category. A demolished wall or a vast heap of builders' material left to disfigure the garden or inconvenience those remaining at home to await the artiste's return home, perhaps after several weeks, is not helpful to those who have to live with it. It was preferable and possible to pay somebody else to do it for you. For quite a few manual labour was something they were more than willing to put behind them. Not for nothing did Artistes refer to the "Profession."

The Artistic Side

Great Art in small rooms was often a watchword: crafts which required attention to detail and painstaking care seem in quite a few cases to have provided lasting interest for several.

George Robey was a maker of violins and enjoyed the friendship of the celebrated Kriesler. It would be sad to think that all those have passed out of existence. Evidence of their whereabouts would be very welcome. The painstaking accuracy and finesse needed to craft such noble instruments can be easily understood.

Little Tich, more correctly Harry Relph, as he preferred to be known, was a skilled painter in water colours. In a time of financial stringency these passed out of the family's hands but seem to have found a safe resting place in the care of a German Professor of Theatre who has an abiding interest and passion for the career and performance of the diminutive comedian. We can be thankful for that.

Sam Barton ("Who almost Rides a Bike") was an inventor of several useful domestic and household appliances, though what these were remains a mystery.

Percy Honri did all the art work for his "Concordia" graceful decorative and eye-catching designs, with, to this observer at least, a remarkable aptness of colour and form to convey an appropriately magical and fairy tale effect.

Mary Honri collected insignia and badges of the military units she visited with E.N.S.A. and made them up as a banner.

Will Hay, noted for his schoolmaster interpretations, gained fame for his work in Astronomy. His telescope was mounted in the roof of his house and it is a thought that the Jewell and Warriss routine involving a telescope, which can detect Venus and other heavenly bodies is switched to observing other forms through the window. ("With my telescope I can see another heavenly body, my little blond cross the road,") may have owed something to Hay's hobby.

Be that as may, Will Hay showed a sense of public duty and used the knowledge involved in his hobby to give lessons in Astronomy and navigation to Air Force cadets during the Second World War. For this work he received an official Government commendation.

Evidence of brain power and clear thinking were evident in Hay's work with the Variety Artistes' Federation, of which he was Chairman for some years.

Walter Lambert, who worked as Lydia Dreams, was the painter of the celebrated "Popularity" scene, showing all the prominent artistes of the pre-1914 era.

Reading

There was plenty of time for reading, though in general this seems to have been mostly given to newspapers.

Barry Ono turned his interest into a hobby for he amassed a remarkable collection of magazines of the Penny Dreadful type, the Literature which dominated the popular field from 1840 until 1900.

In his collection was the world's longest book: 2,028 pages having appeared in 254 weekly 1d editions, entitled "Black Bess or The Knight of the Road," relating the adventures of Dick Turpin. Other titles held were "Jessie, the Mormon's Daughter" (60 weeks in 1860) and "Ned Kelly, or the Ironclad Australian Bushranger," these among many of the staple fare of schoolboys and errand boys. Barry also found time to build up a vast collection of song sheets. As may be imagined, he was very proud of both collections.

Houses

Not unnaturally, with success and increasing prosperity, the thoughts of Artistes turned to acquiring a dwelling reflecting their affluence and as a firm base from which to launch operations. There was a strong impulse to be able to escape from touring and "digs" to somewhere more stable and private. Some indeed became property investors, though not on the American scale.

Percy Honri had a most beautiful house called "Cut Mill" at Bosham, reflecting its owner's style and taste and the position of prestige, respect and eminence he had achieved in the Profession.

Tex McLeod had a farm. And there were many who migrated to the country and the South Coast, attracted no doubt by ease of access to London and the sunshine, as an antidote to the smoke and dreariness of Northern Industrial towns. It was vital to keep healthy and avoid those infections which could cause one to lose one's voice.

"Monsewer" Eddie Gray lived at Shoreham, as did Charlie Austin who ran a guest house ("Charleigh"), right on the coast road.

A large part of the Palladium Crazy Gang migrated to the Sussex Coast, between Worthing and Littlehampton. The train services were fast and frequent and the area was a reasonable drive by car.

Joe O'Gorman Jnr. was the first to find himself a plot (at East Preston), moving later to Barnham, just at the start of the War. Bud Flanagan, Teddy Knox, Horace Reeves and George Black himself were all to be found in the Angmering area.

Some had more money than good taste. One impressario constructed a pile so "Red-brick" that Elsie and Doris Waters, who lived at Steyning, were wont to ask, "Have you seen Tamplin's?" after the well-known chain of public houses along the South Coast.

G. S. Melvin, who lived at Wraysbury on the Thames near Windsor, died from drowning in the river.

Filling in the time

Many activities were used in this respect.

Gus Dale sold Life Insurance to the Profession and also policies against not working. It was quite usual for double acts to insure each other in this way.

Clive Allen, who appeared regularly on the Max Miller bills in the 1950's, had a cafe in Leicester.

Dan Whiteley ran a herbalist's in Kendal. Stainless Stephen who was a school teacher, only working in the school holidays, not full time until his own children had left school and were independent. And there was a comedian who wrote letters to himself at the theatre, to give the impression that he was receiving numerous contracts and offers of work. He was rumbled by his landlady.

The need to be well thought of and have a good reputation was a constant preoccupation. Appearing in the public eye makes the individual so vulnerable to gossip and comment; as we know only too well in these days. In a world where everybody knew everybody else it was virtually impossible to have secrets. The comedian who wrote to himself was merely exhibiting a defence against any suggestion that he was "on the slide." Confidence had to be exhibited and maintained.

General leisure activities

Fishing is regarded as the most popular leisure activity. Harry Tate made it one of his staple sketches of course.

There does not seem to be much evidence that performers were devotees. Except on special occasions. One such fell to Sir Harry Lauder on a visit to Australia in 1937.

At sea, outside Sydney, he landed a 260lb striped marlin, having played the fish for 1½ hours. When landed the trophy was decorated with thistles and illuminated with electric light as a compliment to its captor.

Sir Harry was made an honorary member of the Bermagui Big Game Angling Club and the head was shipped back to Scotland.

Football

Many members of the Profession were interested in football, though often this did not extend far beyond the weekly football coupon. With natural disappointments most often. One syndicate, formed for Pantomime, found itself £20 out of pocket at the end of the run, despite a few small wins.

Several comedians claimed to be players of real skill or eminence, maintaining that only their theatrical activities preventing a career with a professional club.

There was always the possibility of injury to consider. One, for whom dancing was a key part of his livelihood, gave up after one of his own team broke a leg.

A football match on a casual basis, at pantomime time, was quite a well-established tradition.

Foremost of these was the one in Birmingham (lots of Pantomimes and a Mecca of football).

The match in 1939 was noteworthy.

Teams were selected from the Casts of the Alexandra's "Robinson Crusoe" and Prince of Wales's "Cinderella" against Theatre Royal's "Sleeping Beauty." The match was played at Villa Park, the Club's directors being pleased to revive an old tradition.

There was a star-studded and representative turn-out on the field. The Waters Sisters kicked off and Evelyn Laye got the second half going. Tommy Trinder, Tom Gamble, Bunny Doyle, Dave Jackley, Charles Dudley, Jimmy Wheeler, Derek Salberg, Tommy Fitzgibbon and Brian Hayle were among those who risked life and limb in the pouring rain, but several charities were able to benefit. There were many aching limbs and a good deal of stiffness to be worked off in the subsequent days. These jaunts were very good publicity for the various shows.

Southampton Hippodrome bill

Perhaps the most successful of Variety's footballers was Harold Walden, the comedian.

Harold Walden was born in Manchester in 1890. He became a regular soldier with the Cheshire Regiment, attaining the rank of sergeant, serving until in 1911. Halifax Town ("The Shaymen") bought his release from the army so that he could play for them until signing for Bradford City in December 1911. He played for them, with interruptions caused by the war until 1921, when he joined Arsenal.

Harold, who weighed 12 stone and stood 5' 10" was transferred in 1921, for £500.

He also gained a gold medal with the team that won the Olympic title in Stockholm in 1912, in company with Ivan Sharpe, Vivian Woodward and Gordon Hoare – distinguished company.

During the First World War he served in the army again, reaching the rank of captain and played cricket for Spen Victoria and Queensbury C.C.

His off stage versatility was matched by his effective switch in his act from comedy to pathos, with his monologue, "It would do you the world of good ...." "Only me knows why ...." He died in 1955.

A wonderful achievement. A modern parallel would be Colin Grainger of Sheffield Wednesday, who toured the Variety theatres as a crooner, in more modern times.

Treasonable offences

Not everybody filled their time honourably.

The First world War spread its tentacles wide and the temptation to illegal enterprise was strong.

One week at Sunderland, the audience was taking its usual pleasure from one of those turns so necessary to the term Variety.

Sissilatus was a paper cutter, producing figures on request, be it the King or Kitchener, Alf Common, Big Ben or Billy Applegarth.

On one night his snipping attracted the attention of one member of the audience for whom the snips and snaps seemed to fall into the regular patterns of the morse code. A check revealed that this was indeed the case. The coded messages were revealing sailings of ships from Tyne, Tees and Wear. No doubt for onward transmission to the waiting U-boats.

Sissilatus was convicted as a spy and shot at the Tower of London.

It is more than probable that this incident was the basis of the questioning of "The Memory Man" in the film of *The 39 Steps*, joining the performance of an imagined act like Datas, so well-known at that time, to the imagined espionage.

Motoring

The great days of the theatre before 1914 coincided with the rise of the motor car as a popular and available form of transport. and cars can be considered the ideal blend of utility with pleasure.

The Water Rats were soon enthusiastic addicts and organised a run to Brighton. Naturally, vast crowds assembled to see the stars depart. Which they did in high good spirits and noisily, not sparing their criticism of a vehicle which was apparently doomed to remain at the start line, showing no signs of life.

This vehicle was a White Steam car and the delay was caused by the need for the Bunsen burner-type of apparatus under its bonnet to get up steam. And when it did the car sailed off, reaching Brighton and returning without a hitch, which could not be said for most of the others.

Harry Tate of course achieved fame with his "Motoring" sketch and also set the definitive bench mark for personalised number plates, T 8, which says everything. All subsequent efforts pall into insignificance beside it.

Billy Cotton drove racing cars and Roy Barbour had a 3½ litre Jaguar which he used for travelling. In 1940 it was stolen and damaged. Max Miller and George Formby preferred a Rolls Royce and Vic Oliver was able to get from second house at Brighton to a midnight cabaret in London in his. The sparse amount of traffic on the roads in 1930's enabled quite long journeys to be made swiftly.

A danger with night driving is falling asleep at the wheel and Variety Artistes were involved in a number of these accidents.

Cars of those in the Public Eye are a natural target for thieves. Syd Seymour noticed that Dave O'Gorman's car was not in its usual place at Shepherd's Bush Empire. Dave phoned the Police and was surprised and gratified when, 20 minutes later, a message at the Stage Door informed him that his car had been recovered. Apparently its loss was broadcast to "All Cars" and the thieves had drawn up alongside the radio car at traffic lights in Hammersmith!

Festivities

The V.A.F. with its close links to the Water Rats considered a large part of its role as spreading good will and fellowship among its members.

Accordingly the first Federation Day was held at the Crystal Palace, on June 27th, 1907, with, if the hand bill is to be believed, simultaneous gatherings in Berlin, Paris, New York, Cape Town and Sydney.

Doors were open at 9.00 a.m. and a stupendous programme had been drawn up with activities lasting until 10.30 at night when, presumably, even the Crystal Palace Silver Band got tired.

The programme of events was as long it was varied. Music was the background. Grand Organ, Ladies' Orchestra (four times during the day) and Café Chantant formed the background to the dare-devil events: balloon ascents, flying machines, acrobats and high diving, plus swimming and a hat trimming competition for men. There was a concert and a Fun Fair.

In the Grand Variety, one could expect to see Karno's Comedians, Victoria Monks, Sam Mayo, Alf Chester, Athos and Collins, Bella and Bijou, Whit Cunliffe and Malcolm Scott. To make a valid comparison today, it would be like having the Spice Girls, Russ Abbot and Elton John all on view at the same time.

Entertainment for everybody was the aim.

All this provided the background to the Music Hall Athletic Sports Competition.

All events were competed, some very fiercely, but handicap events gave a chance to all. Among those advertised for the 50 yards handicap were Harry Tate, Harry Blake, Geo Mozart, Alec Hurley and Bert Williams.

The chance to get out of doors was evidently appreciated.

Cricket

An interest in watching cricket was a favoured option during the summer months. Manchester, Nottingham, Leeds, Bristol and Bradford were not only good dates but also real cricket centres. And there was ample day time leisure for a visit to the ground.

The famous team for Actors was the Thespids, founded by the lovable Brian Egerton. He had a very good fixture list and the support of Aubrey Smith, later Sir Aubrey.

Pre-1914, the Variety Artistes had a team called the Vaudevillians. Walter Williams played for them, as did Dave and Joe O'Gorman. Walter, who divided his stage career between Music Hall and Musical Comedy, was instrumental in getting the Brothers an invitation to play for the Thespids. In his view, one of the attractions was that, "They play with white stumps!" But it was also a higher standard of play. George Robey was an enthusiast and a competent player of the game who had also, at football, kept goal for Millwall.

Jack Hobbs describes in his book, "My Cricket Memories" how he first played at Lord's for Robey's XI against the Cross Arrows in company with E. G. Hayes, Albert Trott and G. L. Jessop, against E. G. Wynyard, J. W. H. T. Douglas and a whole bevy of the Hearnes, so well-known at Lord's. There are also photos of Robey with the Australian team of 1921 (at practice).

In 1922, a Grand Match was played at Lord's between the Actors and the Variety Artistes.

There was some anxiety about the strength of the Variety side, the Actors, by virtue of education and background, having a potentially much stronger team. Dave O'Gorman, a very capable and determined opening bat and Joe O'Gorman were soon recruited. Joe, a slow bowler, stressed the need for a really competent wicket keeper, as this was a proper and not a joke match. When asked whether he knew of one said he did, called ANDY ANDY, a ventriloquist. This was in fact Andy Kempton, who had been a Surrey Professional and was Joe's team mate at Honor Oak C.C. and was Jack Hobbs' business partner in his shop in Fleet Street.

The celebrities duly gathered at Lord's and entered into the spirit of the day.

Albert Whelan, an Australian was recruited together with Billy Merson, who said he would give £50 to Charity if he could be the opening bowler. His request was agreed to and at lunch he stated further that he would jump in the fountain for £5, which prompted another comedian to remark that for another fiver he would drink the water.

The match proceeded on an even keel until Joe O'Gorman's bowling, with help from Andy Andy, decided matters for the Variety Artistes.

In fact, Joe did the hat trick. His three victims being Martin Lewis, who had played for Kent, Reggie Crawford, brother of Jack Crawford of Surrey and England and, lastly, Aubrey Smith who hit up a catch to Reggie Sharland, father of David Croft, who is also very keen on the game.

Andy Kempton was so pleased with all this that he presented Joe with the ball duly mounted and inscribed, "Presented to J. G. O'Gorman Esq. who with this ball took 7 wickets for 32 runs, including the hat trick at Lord's September 5th 1922. From Andy Andy. Well bowled."

Other notables playing in this game, for the Actors, included Gerald Du Maurier, Basil Rathbone, Willy Bruce and Desmond Roberts.

In more modern times, Leslie Crowther has been known for his keen attendance at Lord's and involvement in the Lord's Taverners' work for Charity.

Roy Castle has shown more than average talent. He played for Lord's Taverners against old England in 1963, scoring 22 not out. A talented man.

Derek Salberg of the Alex Birmingham was a notable cricket enthusiast and a supporter of Warwickshire.

Harry Roy was another enthusiast. In 1935, he arranged eight fixtures in the London area for his band which was, no doubt, good publicity.

THE POLITICS OF THE BUSINESS

Variety folk were involved in a risky and chancy profession. Time for talking was readily available, not simply gossip but about the difficulties, often pressing ones, involved in making a living on the stage.

To tell the story of the organisation of disparate societies; The Terriers and others which were not functioning very well into the Variety Artistes' Federation is not being attempted here. But the organisation's close links with the Water Rats gave it a social aspect, with good fellowship and relaxation as desirable ends.

Fellow feeling and conviviality were essential requirements for membership.

The Water Rats and the Lady Ratlings, organised by Noelle Damerell, had benevolence well on their mind, with fund-raising as an objective, notably through the medium of the Annual Water Rats Ball, where one may suspect there was a strong element of see and be seen.

Such a manifestation had disastrous consequences for the notorious Dr. Crippen, who had Ethel Neve there as his partner. The sharp-eyed Mrs. Paul Martinetti observed, "That girl has got Belle Elmore's jewellery on." And in consequence further enquiries were made with the consequent pursuit and arrest of Crippen.

There was also the Water Rats' Matinée, usually at the London Pavilion, which was a show case and opportunity for some lesser-known acts to make an impression. The list of participants reads like a professional Roll of Honour.

Cover and centre spread
The programme for the G.O.W.R. matinee at The London Pavilion, 19 November, 1906

Trips and excursions were a great feature of the early days of the Water Rats, taking place every two or three weeks. Polhill near Sevenoaks by coach driven by Tom Brantford and river excursions by train to Staines, followed by a reserved pleasure steamer to Marlow or Windsor were part of a regular programme. And a river trip to the "Magpie" Sunbury-on-Thames was involved with the actual founding of the Water Rats.

Stunts, involving "rescues" of "drowning" swimmers and incompetent oarsmen who obligingly caught a crab as the steamer passed by were a regular feature. Jack O'Connor and Charlie Mildare are recorded as strong swimmers on these occasions. They would need to be in the Thames.

For general out-of-doors activity, the Annual V.A.F. Garden Party and sports were eagerly awaited highlights.

Accomplished Club Cricketers:
The O'Gorman brothers at The Oval nets in 1926

GOLF

The activity which attracted most participation on a long term basis, offering fresh air, social contact and an element of competition for the participants was Golf.

The Profession got hooked on Golf in a big way in the years leading up to the First World War. Much of the impetus for this came from the American Artists who were coming over in large numbers just about then.

Alfredo, Charlie O'Donnell, Jess Jacobsen, Charlie Tucker were prominent among these, being much above the average standard, being willing, in the American way, to put in the necessary serious approach and practice.

The new activity did not meet with the approval of all. George Gilbey, the celebrated Clown, was heard to declare seeing young Joe O'Gorman at Crewe with his bag said, "Gor Blimey, look what this business is coming to!"

But the obvious attractions of the game to people with ample day time leisure could not be denied. Many of the provincial courses were sparsely used during the week.

But the Americans certainly set the standard at first. Causing not a little frustration to those who found that the game did not come as easily as they expected. Like the one who, returning to Waterloo from a disastrous round, threw his whole bag and clubs from the bridge into the Thames. And went out and bought a completely new set the next morning.

The Vaudeville Golfing Society was soon in operation, owing much of its early vitality to Billy Merson who was a good and enthusiastic player. He was largely instrumental in getting the V.G.S. affiliations and concessions at many of the best and appropriate clubs in the provinces and London: Fulwell, Sudbury, St. Augustine's Ramsgate, Moor Allerton Leeds, Cardiff and 50 others around the country, at some of which the V.G.S. members could play free.

It must be confessed that not all Artistes conformed with the Etiquette of the game. One anxious to get on with his round, seeing a very portly player ahead and thinking it to be J. W. Rickaby (a sizeable figure) yelled out, "Hi fat guts! Move your a ...."

Ten minutes later the Steward arrived with the player's green fee and the Secretary's compliments to remove himself from the course.

The rotund player ahead had been Lord Castlerosse.

The V.G.S. did not play there again.

And another player, an American, currently involved in a scandalous divorce case was, at about the third, also asked to remove himself from the course. He had been warned not to appear but took no notice. This was at Wimbledon.

By the 1930's, the Society was well-established and regular matches and competitions were being played; the Billy Merson Shield (the oldest event), the Tom Arnold Bowl and the Apollo Cup.

It is recorded that Carl Baliol beat the pro, Fred Cox 3 and 1 at Chigwell, a match against the Essex Professionals and was rated just about the best player in the Business.

James Foreman, Captain for that year 1933, shot 66 at Molesey Hurst, which was pleasing as he had been dejected about his game. Frank Radcliffe scored 63, 12 under par at Yelverton, a course very handy for the Palace Plymouth.

Donald Peers, Dave Carter and Peter Fannan are recorded as playing regularly at this time.

The participants obviously believed in having a good day. In 1937, on a beautiful sunny day at Thorndon Park, the match against the Professionals was only lost on the last green. But the company then repaired to supper and the second house at the Holborn Empire. That sounds like a very good day!

Matches were played against the Stage GS. and Billy Bennett and Charlie Naughton presented a trophy, the Berkshire Bowl, for long handicap players.

All this was supervised by the long-serving Secretary, J. Alex Rose, who announced that lapel badges were available for 6s 6d and the Dinner was always liable to be heavily subscribed.

By the early 1950's there were 180 members and the list is a veritable roll of honour, for it included so many celebrated names, especially comedians:-

Arthur Askey, Harry Bailey, Issy Bonn, Peter Brough, Albert Burdon, Charlie Chester, George Doonan, Alec Finlay, Bud Flanagan, Eddie Gray, Dickie Henderson, Arthur Haynes, Nat Jackley, Jimmy Jewell and Ben Warris, Teddy Knox, Johnny Lockwood, all the Crazy Gang, Joe O'Gorman, Vic Oliver, Frank Randle, Al Read, Leslie Sarony, Max Wall and Jimmy Wheeler.

Max Miller does not seem to have been a member but he was not known for joining things. But his skill as a player is testified to by many. The match against the Stage G.S. in June 1947 was lost 5-7 and the line up may be taken as representative of those turning out in matches at that time. Two very prominent players, Ted Ray and Donald Peers, were chosen to play Bob Hope and Bing Crosby on their visit here in 1952, beating them 2 and 1.

The O'Gorman brothers golfing at Carnoustie in 1934

Crosby said he wasn't too worried and looked forward to playing a return at Palm Springs where, no doubt, the weather would be better.

Handicaps listed for 1947 included Jimmy Green 6; Bob Beamand and Merv Saunders 8; Sid Jerome, John Lockwood and Jack Leonard 20; Eugene Pini and Syd Harrison 24.

There is no doubt that the V.G.S. was a flourishing and well-run organisation which played a prominent part in the lives of many. Great credit must be given to the efficient and long-serving Secretary, J. Alex Rose.

HORSE RACING

With many afternoons at their disposal, Variety Artistes were patrons of the Turf. Some indeed owned race horses with varying success, sometimes without appreciating the enormous cost involved.

Dave Carter, the Irish tenor ("Love me and the world is mine") was self-appointed "Bookmaker to the Profession" and took a regular advert in "The Performer" to this effect. Flanagan and Allen's plan to try their hand at bookmaking is well-documented.

Naturally performers were not unknown to the Racing Men and other habitués of the courses. Joe O'Gorman Senior and a friend were attending the Derby and stopped by a Wheel of Fortune side-show, where it was obvious that the wheel was being stopped on purpose on numbers which carried no bets. Joe pointed this out in a loud voice to his companion and was rewarded by a savage kick from behind on his ankle. As he turned and limped away, he was supported by a most sympathetic man, who whispered to him the while, "Now then Joe, we don't come in to the Canterbury and give you the bird while you are working, so let's all get on without any interference. Okay?"

Ted Waite, brother of the unctuous comic singer, J. W. Rickaby, was a great one for horse races. Having spent the week at Newmarket with Sam Bell, attending the meeting every day, they found themselves at the end of the week with not a penny between them. There was the hotel bill to consider but they still wanted to bet.

Waite was struck by a bright idea. He thought that Sam could pawn his false teeth, some of which were gold. They did this and reached the Heath in time for the first race and finished several pounds to the good. So they booked a taxi back to town and Waite ordered two steaks and waited for Bell to return from the pawnbroker. Unfortunately, he found it closed.

The well-known tipster "Prince Monolulu" was a regular attender at variety theatres, without his feather head dress, but was a rather disruptive presence as he was accustomed to burst out laughing at the wrong time, so drawing attention to himself and distracting from the stage show.

But the greatest enthusiast, and perhaps the most consistent loser, was Fred Curran, a singer of parodies; a very jovial and humorous man, always good company. He would come to breakfast in the digs, chanting in his sonorous voice, "Oh I'm going to the races today. I'll have the bookmakers begging for mercy. They will be paying my expenses for the week."

Sadly it was Fred who did the paying and, naturally, he never learned. It was Fred Curran who referred to a particularly obnoxious theatrical wife as "the Yard Dog."

The Turf was as much of a Siren to performers as to others.

Ernest Shand (1868 1924)

Ernest Shand, who was born Ernest William Watson, had apart from his appearances on the Halls, a second accomplishment: his virtuosity on the guitar at which he achieved notable fame and respect as performer and composer.

Coming from a musical background – his father taught him violin and his mother the piano - he sang in the church choir at Holy Trinity, Hull and won a Music Scholarship to Hull Grammar School. But he was looking for something more original and so took up the guitar.

He was a pupil of Madame Sydney Pratten, but she considered him far ahead of her in accomplishment. When she died (1895), Shand composed Funeral March No. 88 in her honour and further compositions followed: Guitar Concerto No. 100 and his Improved Method for the Guitar, which became the standard work of instruction. He did much to popularise the instrument and to move away from the influence of Banjoism.

He wrote Opus 48, the first guitar concerto by a British composer, which Julian Bream later added to his repertoire. Shand supported Barnes and Mullins in their efforts to establish a guitar, mandolin and banjo society.

These successes prompted Shand to leave the Variety stage and devote himself to his chosen instrument. Despite critical acclaim and some successful concerts, he was not able to do sufficiently well to continue with it and he returned to the Variety stage.

He continued to compose but his health was not good and he eventually died in Birmingham on 20th November 1924.

THEY HAVE THEIR EXITS

It is, one may suppose, well known that Tommy Cooper, Eric Morecombe, Billy Russell and Arthur Lucan, among others, all passed away in harness, as the saying goes, either at the side of the stage or awaiting their turn. For an actor this may be seen as appropriate a leave taking as may be desired.

But other exits, some no less dramatic in their way, reveal much of the impact, effect and memory performers have left behind. So while it must not be said that nothing in their lives became them like the leaving of it, quite often things about performers became apparent which were not so before.

Wal Pink

Wal Pink, the celebrated script writer of so many West End revues and Harry Tate's sketches, was regarded as the keenest intellect in the Business. His influence in the formation of the Water Rats and V.A.F. was paramount. His strength and convictions were of untold value in the difficult days of the Strike (1907) and his opinion was always the deciding factor in procedural or policy matters.

His popularity was unsurpassed. He did not knock people and showed total honesty and integrity to go with his sound practical commonsense.

He wrote songs, sketches and revues and was instrumental in making the reputation of a large number of performers. Wal came from Devon and, from early years, seemed possessed of a very keen sense of humour, perhaps inherited from his father.

Apparently, the young Wal had a trick of jumping up and kicking his own behind. He asked his father, "Can you do that?" and his father replied, "Yes, TURN ROUND!"

His wit was legendary.

A comic declared he had got a new act. "Oh yes," replied Wal, "whose is it?"

Mr Wal Pink

Another was distraught as his wife had run off with a coloured artiste and enquired what he should do. "Black up and win her back again."

His inventive wit was seldom at rest. He kept the wall next to his bed painted clean white and a pencil placed just below. This was in case he had an idea and could write it down at once and avoid the risk of having forgotten it in the morning.

His passing was in character. A revue at Sheffield was not having a successful time. Wal was summoned as Trouble Shooter, the universal cure for failing shows and left at once when called, driving to Yorkshire, in appalling weather in an open car and arriving late at night. A rehearsal was called immediately after the second house. The dire situation meant work had to go on until the early hours. Cold when he arrived and sitting in damp clothes in a theatre growing colder by the minute, enabled an infection to set in, from which he died on 27th October 1922.

His funeral tribute reaffirmed that the world was a better pace for his presence. He exemplified the words of the Water Rats' Ritual, which he had largely written:

"Rectitude and Righteousness;
"Amiability and Advancement;
"Truth and Trustfulness;
"Straightforwardness and Strength."

His character was an example to all. He made his exit far too soon but cherished by those who were close to him and, indeed, the whole Profession.

Joe Elvin

Joe Elvin, originally working with his father as Keegan and Elvin, celebrated sketch artistes, was a real personality.

Joe Elvin's passing gave rise to a considerable correspondence in the theatrical press, with memories of the act, before it was famous, appearing at the TCP circuit (Taverns, Clubs and Pubs).

One writer remembers in particular the sketch "Poor Joe." The idea is that Poor Joe is on the way to visit his mother's grave, struggling against his own physical weakness and the extreme bitterness of the winter weather, with snow falling and a bitter wind driving the scudding clouds across the night sky, obscuring the moon and intensifying the atmosphere. The moon was a candle in a lantern and the "clouds," gauzes moved across it to signify the gust-driven storm wrack.

As Joe stumbles towards the cemetery he is overcome with weakness and collapses at the entrance. After a suitable pause, the moon appropriately appearing and disappearing, a friendly policeman appears and naturally wants to know what is wrong.

Poor Joe confesses his weakness and the bobby suggests a swig from his flask, carried by all constables on night duty, supposedly hot coffee but usually something a good deal stronger. But the fortifying liquid is unable to sustain the ailing man and he expires on the cemetery steps, "Poor Joe."

The sketch naturally milked the melancholy atmosphere and melodramatic pathos for all it was worth. But at times the effect was dissipated by the policeman walking to the side of the stage and urging the prop boy in an all too audible stage whisper to, "Keep that bloody moon moving."

Mr Joe Elvin with Pat O'Gorman

Later on Wal Pink wrote for Joe Elvin, such celebrated sketches as "Toffy's Trotter," recalling his enthusiasm for the Turf and the origin of the Water Rats and the trotting pony of that name.

The fraternity known as The Racing Men were all known to Joe and he to them. Liberality and open-handedness among the punters always being welcome to the habitués of the Turf.

Joe was known for his fondness for a bet. He was one of those of whom it could be said that he would bet on raindrops running down a window pane.

As, finally, Joe fell on hard times, the Profession rallied round to give a Benefit Performance. This duly took place, was very well-supported and a most useful sum was raised to be given to Joe.

Joe O'Gorman vetoed this, knowing that it would soon be dissipated among cronies in various hostelries. O'Gorman's proposal was that the money be invested and Elvin should be given an income, the Principal reverting to the Variety Artistes' Benevolent Fund on his death and that Elvin should live in Joe O'Gorman's house in Vine Road, Barnes, where he was accommodated with bed and board. He was an enthusiastic trencherman and ordinarily, when called to the table was accustomed to declare, "Yes. I'm under starter's orders." And, when asked if he would like any more to eat, "No thank you, I've bolted."

This scheme was duly carried out. But as a correspondent pointed out, there was a rump of associates ever ready to help Joe spend his allowance at the pub, The Red Rover on Barnes Common.

There Joe would stay until past lunch time, eventually leaving to stagger across the grass and home for his meal.

Of course, he had to respect the wishes of his benefactor's wife, Lil O'Gorman, with regard to time and she was not too pleased to have her domestic arrangements disturbed. Joe was delayed as much by his liking for "Just-another half" as fear for the lady's more than forceful personality.

Eventually Joe had to turn his steps homeward.

The lunch was turning frigid on the table and Joe was conspicuous by his absence.

Eventually he would totter into view. Lil's scorn knew no bounds. "Here he comes the drunken old bugger" and he would enter to take his place in a deathly silence, no welcoming bottle of Bass at his place. Joe was in disgrace – yet again.

The situation was usually resolved by Pat, Joe O'Gorman's youngest son asking whether Uncle Joe could have a bottle of beer.

Joe Elvin's response was to declare, "Pat, you're a Prince" which cleared the air with a laugh and all was forgiven – until the next time.

Joe Elvin had the capacity to inspire friendship and affectionate memories, by his performances and his personality.

Sam Mayo
The Immobile One

Sam Mayo had a dry wit, a sardonic sense of humour and was impatient and critical of those in authority. He never minded voicing his opinion. Not unnaturally he was impatient of criticism directed at him. His performances were based on an enviable minimalism. His make-ups were of the simplest. For his song, "Ladies don't be frightened, I'm an Indian" he merely donned a dressing gown and stuck two chicken feathers in his hair.

He sang in a nasal monotone, devoid of gesture, movement or mannerism, as befitted his Bill Matter.

> "Ladies don't be frightened I'm an Indian;
> I come from Timbuctoo, three, four, five, six.
> The day I sailed away it was a windy 'un;
> Be careful girls, I'm full of Indian tricks!"

He would follow this with one or more of his own compositions and then leave for another hall, moving rapidly no doubt, for he had the reputation of working more theatres in one night than any other performer.

He was also a prolific song writer. For himself, "I never stopped running until I got home;" "She cost me 7/6;" "When I woke up in the morning;" "I only came down for the day."

As a writer of songs, Sam Mayo's wit and perception were invaluable ingredients. Revue was the really up-to-the-minute form of entertainment in 1914. So his observations of the requirements needed, "... if you want to get on in revue," were timely, apposite and absolutely on the mark.

"Keep a smile on your face; show a little bit of lace; if you want to get on in revue."

But the ditty goes on to warn that, even if your admirer has a car with a seat "… as big as a sofa,"

"You are safer with the chauffeur – if you want to get on in revue!"

The sub-text of just how far a respectable, or not so respectable girl, might be asked or expected to go, in order to make progress in her career would have struck the mark as a knowing and pertinent observation of the follies, foibles and perils of a theatrical life.

Sam was of the same generation as Wal Pink and shared his love of a wager. A characteristic large-heartedness was shown in his organisation of a matinée for "The Racecourse Employees Benevolent Fund;" a fairly extensive but undeserving body one would have thought. Especially so in Sam's case as he had already donated a goodly part of his earnings to them over the years in any case. But the event was held and proved a satisfactory success.

Sam died in 1938 while making a shot at Billiards, he was an expert player, only a week after the funeral of his son.

He was lamented by a large following.

Charlie Coburn

One of the long-lived stars, surviving from his days as the singer of "The Man who Broke the Bank at Monte Carlo" until 1945.

His passing gave rise to a tribute of an unusual sort; a letter to "The Performer."

"In my youth I showed promise at my scholar and was diligent at my studies and, being of a serious turn of mind, it came to be understood that I would offer myself as a candidate for the Ordained Ministry.

However, I fell in with a fast set who cared only for a life of pleasure and enter-tainment. My studies and aim in life were all but forgotten.

One evening I was taken aside by a courteous elderly man who said, "Young man, this life you are leading will get you nowhere and cause all your expectations to be disap-pointed. You should get yourself free of these people who have probably already cost a great deal of money and taken up again a regular life and the studies you have neglected.

Chastened by his words, I resumed my calling and am now ordained Minister and active in the work.

My unknown benefactor was none other than Charlie Coburn to whom I owe a profound debt of gratitude."

This memorial tribute goes far to show that Variety performers were not the witless, unthinking, feckless people they are often made out to be, but, in many cases, discerning, observant and appreciative of a fuller and orderly life, very often with a passionate belief in the value of Education as the pathway to a better and fuller life.

George Robey's son became a Judge, Sir Edward Robey: Jimmy Gold's son became a catholic priest: Gilly Potter's boy was J. H. B. Peel, for many years the Countryside and Wild Life correspondent for the "Daily Telegraph." Others were doctors, teachers, lawyers with solid professional careers as a protection against the cruel uncertainties of the Stage.

Fred Barnes
"The black sheep of the family"

We have big Stars nowadays. The Crooners who had the ladies swooning and screaming, especially in the 1950's are a well attested phenomenon.

Fred Barnes received similar adulation in his heyday, the years running up to and including the First World War. He was the premier light comedian of the Halls. With his photogenic looks, his fair hair, his impeccable dress sense and his elegant charm, he was the focus of all attention. His stage presence radiated.

His bill matter, "The Black Sheep of the Family" and his songs, ""There's a Friend on Every Milestone," "Dirty Little Hand," "Floating with my Boating Girl," "The Ragtime Violin" and "Give me the Moonlight" made him a top attraction. He should be considered one of the Greats.

He was one of the few Music Hall Artistes permitted to appear on the bill at the London Coliseum with "The Divine" Sarah Bernhardt.

Fred Barnes in 1910

He was one of the first men to play Principal Boy in Pantomime. Fred revelled in the limelight. He played up to the crowds at the stage door and was more than willing to acknowledge those who recognised him in the street.

He adopted an extravagant life style. He was, perhaps, somewhat spoiled by his success. He was soon the owner of the first of a series of Rolls Royce cars. He might have been the examplar of the expression, "If you've got it, flaunt it." But not all his attitudes were acceptable to the popular mind, especially in those pre-Wolfenden days.

His proclivity led hostility to boil over and, at Finsbury Park, his car was defaced with FREDA painted on it.

The resulting scandal led to the downward path. Scandalous behaviour was regarded as a bad Box Office risk.

Fred disappeared into obscurity and, by the late thirties, was playing the piano in a public house in Southend.

His companion demanded the larger share if not all of the few shillings Fred was able to earn. His situation does not seem to have been at all comfortable.

Eventually he was found dead in his indigent lodgings, his head turned towards the gas fire, though the gas was not turned on.

A £1 note was found inside his sock.

Arthur Prince and Jim

It is well known that props are an essential part of the Variety Artiste's stock in trade. But it was reckoned that a prop had to be a help and not a hindrance, once used, that is useful throughout the time on the stage, part of the whole "make up;" hat, coat, trousers, boots, wig and face.

Jimmy Nervo of the Crazy Gang, was reckoned to be a supreme master in prop handling.

The ventriloquist's doll is the definitive prop. There is no act without it and vents fall broadly into two categories; brilliant technicians and those whose voice projecting skills are, to say the least, sketchy but whose act is highly amusing, but of limited technical proficiency.

This situation was clearly expressed by Dave Poole, who when asked how long it took to work up a vent act like his, replied "Like mine? Now!"

But the vent's alter ego, his doll, has to have some existence of its own, to provide some reason for the offering. The creation of a credible foil has been diverse, for without a lively vitality there is no act.

Their names spring readily to mind; Coster Joe, Augustus Peabody, Emu, Hodge, Jerry Fisher, Archie Andrews, Snodgrass.

It was Jerry Fisher who was made to sing:

"I'm Jerry Fisher, one of the gold gilitia,
I'm one of the rank and file,
No wonder the ladies smile,
I'm only a wooden soldier."

Arthur Prince on a 1911 Variety Bill at The Palace, Shaftesbury Avenue

No bother for him about bottles of beer for his best brother's birthday!

By common consent the closest affinity between vent and doll was between Arthur Prince and "Jim."

When Arthur Prince passed away this verse tribute was published in the Performer.

"I quickened to his touch,
He gave me breath
His fingers moved my puppet lips.
Now he has gone the floats are dimmed by death
And side by side we lie in mute eclipse.
In him alone I lived and moved and spoke,
You who remain may voice your sorrowing love.
No words alas, can humble Jim evoke

To mourn the passing of his pal above.
Though yet in silence I must go below
And leave this life upon the ocean wave,
There is a Glory on me as I go.
Oh! Lucky Jim to share a Prince's grave."

This tribute from a member of the Public has a remarkable poignancy. In reality it was Arthur Prince who had a life on account of his creation.

Jim earned him his living. And one who was entertained, no doubt frequently, by the act has been moved to express his gratitude for the share he was able to take in the bond of sympathy between Prince and his boy. It so often takes a death to provoke the strongest and most clearly felt experiences.

Jack O'Connor

With Jack O'Connor, yet another from the Roll of Honour of Liverpool comedians, one is clutching at straws. He died cruelly young and not much has been written about him, but we have the testimony of those who did remember his engaging personality and lovable nature. He worked the act Jack and Evelyn with consistent and increasing success in the years leading up to the First World War. His progress in the years he worked, was restricted by two weaknesses. His youth and his fondness for beverages stronger than lemonade.

The bookers reckoned they could easily get him three figures (£100 a week) but for his youth and youthful appearance. It is a demonstrable feature that audiences will not laugh so readily at young people. A deal of worldy wisdom is required to give depth and maturity to a comedian's observations and jests. Neither Feste nor Lear's Fool would have been young men.

He had a ready, keenly observant and spontaneous wit.

At that period American acts had a habit of advertising themselves using a number, as FAY, TWO COLEYS and FAY and we all know the FOUR COHANS.

Jack O'Connor saw Joe O'Gorman struggling with a suitcase in each hand at Euston Station and said, "Oh look. It's JOE, TWO BAGS AND JOE."

Jack was helped in his act by his sister, Evelyn, who was a person of immense loyalty, charm and determination. She would make light of Jack's weakness make sure he was presentable, feed him his lines, ensuring that the act never faltered, cover up for him and assist him to the limit of sisterly love and beyond it.

Many tried to help him, especially those Roman Catholic priests who made chaplaincy to the theatre one of their pastoral responsibilities.

But ultimately it was all to no avail and another victim was claimed by a curse so often fatally attractive to those whose role in life is to amuse other people: at what cost to their self esteem and nervous constitution, when the public house is just around the corner, we may only imagine.

Anyway Jack O'Connor was a magnificent performer and much imitated.

As with many other of artistic talent one is left to regret that he did not live longer to display it.

Basil Hallam

The story of Basil Hallam has been very influential in my interest in the passing of performers.

He illustrates a slice of social history of the period, before 1914, which disappeared in the maelstrom of the First World War.

This era gave rise to a style of young men known, collectively, as the (K)nuts.

They were distinguished by a languid, affected, though polished and refined manner. They delighted in the easy manipulation of canes and monocles, were impeccably tailored and kept their hair in place with a quantity of Brilliantine.

They studiously avoided exercise and were most at home in casual lounging.

However, the style was not unpleasing for they aimed to be refined and elegant towards ladies.

The first flower of this type was Basil Hallam. He personified the type precisely.

In 1915 he was appearing with Nelson Keys, Gwendoline Brogden and Elsie Janis in "The Passing Show" at the Palace, London.

His song "Gilbert the Filbert" celebrated the (K)nut.

> "I'm Gilbert the Filbert the Nut with the "K"
> the pride of Piccadilly, the blasé roué,
> Oh Hades the ladies would leave their wooden huts,
> For Gilbert the Filbert, the Colonel of the Knuts."

The song was on everybody's lips.

Basil Hallam, 1915

However, this was not to the taste of all with War fever at its height and slackers having white feathers pinned to their lapels. And a claque of those in uniform got in to the theatre to heckle Hallam over his failure to join up and his guying of those who were in Khaki.

He got the Bird.

However, unbeknown to his persecutors Hallam *had* volunteered at the start of the War, only to be found unfit. The Authorities were more particular then than later.

But the criticism worried Hallam badly and he volunteered for the only branch that would take him, the Balloon Corps.

This was War service at its most hazardous. Captive balloons were hoisted to spot targets for the Artillery and observe enemy movement generally. They were a choice target themselves, though an equally hazardous one. Special incendiary bullets were used against them. When hit the gas exploded instantly.

Basil Hallam met his death in this way. Man's inhumanity to man. Has a popular song ever caused a death before or since?

Alec Navarre

Alec Navarre, an Australian, starting as a single turn about 1935 had reached a prominent position by the outbreak of hostilities.

He received good notices for his fine impressions of such diverse singers as Chaliapin, Chevalier, John MacCormack, all leavened with gentle humour and intimate manner-isms, plus effective harmonica playing from time to time. A good solid act with a touch of distinction about it.

The start of the Second World War produced a whole set of strange conditions, among them the closing of all theatres and places of amusement in fear of heavy casu-alties from bombing.

This decision was reversed quite soon but the Blitz and raids on provincial towns did make life extremely hazardous.

Some performers were easily frightened. After one raid on London the manager of a theatre received a telegram from an artiste saying he was too ill to appear. The telegram had been sent from Northampton!

Another refused to go to Newcastle as the train might be shelled from the North Sea!

One comedian, young enough to have been serving in the Forces, tried to avoid his fire-watching duties as he had a perforated eardrum!

Birmingham, with its industry and Coventry, proved main targets, the raids coming in waves. Usually it was possible to predict the time of raids from the flying time from bases in France or Low Countries. But attacks on Birmingham were a bit unpredict-able. One night they were later than usual and Alec Navarre was killed in his digs on the Pershore Road. One of the chorus ladies in the same show, "Folies de Minuit" being the only survivor in the house, finding herself, after the explosion, on the roof. (14th October 1940).

Conditions were demanding and hazardous. One member of the cast of the revue packed his bags and left, saying he was getting out while he could still sing the song which made him famous!

His departure and Navarre's regretted and untimely death left the show short of running time but Low and Webster who were appearing at the Hippodrome Aston filled in, doing the journey twice and dodging the bombs on the way. This was one occasion when turn working was allowed in the Provinces. The show had to go on. Navarre's exit had given them a chance, based on extremely unfortunate circumstances.

If Navarre had not in fact died in harness, his passing was, to say the least, unusual.

George Robey

The Alexandra Theatre, Birmingham, 1938/9. Almost an exit.

The "Alec" Pantomime in Birmingham was regarded as one of the flagship showcases for traditional mid-winter fare. To appear in it was regarded as a mark of approval and confirmation of recognition of a performer's status as being of the right pedigree, at the top of the Pantomime tree and, for some, the summit of their ambition.

The Salbergs who ran the theatre were very conscious of their status and indeed their responsibility to their public. By skilful use of forward planning they had heavy bookings from works' outings, social clubs, schools and other bodies well in hand, even before the next season's title or main artistes had even been announced. There could be nothing sub-standard or second rate. The patrons knew what they wanted and what to expect.

In the latter 1930's the Alec had seen among others, Clarkson Rose, Georgie Wood, Barry Lupino, Billy Merson, Hal Bryan and Sandy Powell, all Panto luminaries to lead the comedy.

MR. GEORGE ROBEY.

It was a bold and expensive venture. The opening was so successful as to surpass expectations. Robey was full of inspiration and attack, a resourceful veteran with surprising vigour, inspiring all the company.

Then disaster struck.

On the fourth afternoon of the run, Robey fell from the stage to the stalls. His vision had been impaired by the mask he was wearing for a new exit.

Despite his heavy fall he was back on the stage in an instant, his trouper's instinct immediately coming in to effect. He got through the performance, though he was in great pain, but it was his last show for nearly three months. He had broken three ribs, injured his spine and bruised his face. So great was the force of his fall that he broke the arm of the seat in the front row. It has been written that he had over-imbibed, which was absolutely not true.

This was a real crisis for the show and for the new Manager. But the show must go on and all rallied round splendidly. Replacements were brought in: Renée Houston and Donald Stewart; the Diamond Brothers; The Three Loose Screws. Chic Elliott cleaned the black from her face and became Mrs. Crusoe for the duration. But she too fell ill.

George Hirste, well known for his Dame roles, was summoned from London. He arrived on the noon train and played the matinée at 2.30.

The pantomime lived down its shocking bad luck and ran for seventeen weeks, giving the box office its usual busy time.

So Robey's exit might have proved fatal. That it did not was Providential but it provided opportunities for others and demonstrated, yet again the capacity of the theatre and its participants to be vitalised and surprising in their response to Life's Final Curtain.

THE LATTER DAYS
AT HOLBORN

The Royal Holborn, its former title, was, despite a favourable position at the heart of London's busy thoroughfares, adjoining business houses and lawyers' offices, something of a white elephant until Walter Gibbons took it over and opened it as the Holborn Empire.

He started a policy of "Lightning Variety" with 18 or 20 turns, twice nightly, with the artistes being allowed very little time on the stage and certainly none allowed to leave to make a change, when the audience had nothing to watch.

The regime to enforce this could be fierce. Dora Lyric was asked, to save time, to delete a chorus, which left her only a verse and chorus to sing. It was a case of making an immediate impression or failing: emphasising George Robey's words, "In the music hall it is no good finessing. You have to hit them on the head."

Sometimes, despite the genius of the stage manager, Billy Whitmore, in getting the turns on and off, there were confusions. Sinclair and Whiteford did not make their appearance until after midnight and, not caring to have their act called "Alone in London," the patrons having left to catch their trains, sued, successfully, for a 12th of their salary, on the grounds that they were playing a matinée!

Max Miller in one of his magnificently gaudy costumes

But the theatre soon became a Mecca and a popular one, with public, artistes and critics.

"I like the Holborn Empire. It looks like music hall. It is always crowded and companionable and full of people who mean to laugh .... There should be a Royal Performance at the Holborn. The Holborn is a real music hall with and audience to match (1935). And:

"There is more of the old time atmosphere at the Holborn than in any other house in London. The Palladium is too grand; the Victoria Palace too respectable; the Pavilion too non-stop; the Garrick too self-conscious. The acts that go best at Holborn are the traditional variety acts." (1936)

These flattering comments draw attention to the very wide range of potential audience the Variety Halls had to encompass. Striking the balance between progress and tradition and improvement was no easy matter; but then it never is.

The regret for times past and the trend towards "refinement" or having a modern and acceptable style was summed up by the comedian who declared, in a moment of confrontation with the management, "This business started going to the dogs when the comedians started to clean their finger nails!" One can see what he meant but trends and ranges of options grow apace as the Thirties got under way.

The range soon extended to American bands and Film Stars. Their booking to appear in England did not pass without controversy and one can detect a well-defined strand of anti-American and anti-foreign feeling, in the Press at least.

A letter from an artiste to "The Performer" of July 1935 protests about a foreign act being allowed to "turn-work" that is to appear at more than one hall a night – a practice which was forbidden in the Provinces – so causing a British act to lose a week's work.

However, Louis Armstrong, appearing in 1933, indicated that the trend for American performers was not going to diminish, despite some unfavourable comments.

His personality was judged too bizarre for the public to take to their hearts and "..... a London audience gets tired of Armstrong, for, as it stands his act is too long. There is too much striving after effect, too many antics, too many top notes."

It was a reported that a number of people walked out, being tired of 75 high C's and incessant rompings.

His act was characterised as 50 per cent showmanship, 50 per cent instrumental cleverness and 0 per cent music.

The "Daily Telegraph" reported it was not everybody's idea of music. It found no rhythm or melody. There was more melody in a barrel organ.

These are harsh words. The "News of the World" was even more outspoken, "If this is what England wants, God save England."

A surprising comment from the "Melody Maker," "the sensational panders to base emotions."

On March 13th, 1939, Holborn had a bill with Lucan and McShane, Cyril Fletcher, Boy Foy, Dave and Joe O'Gorman and Jack Hylton and his Band. Among the Band's personnel was a young Ernie Wise who, no doubt, was imbibing and learning lessons which were to stand him in good stead.

Bebe Daniels in a white tulle Hartnell gown at The Holborn Empire, 1940

By the end of the decade, the Holborn had extended its range to encompass "Productions," spectacular revues similar to those which had been running at the Palladium.

A longer show with its spectacular chorus effects gave the leading performers the chance to do more spots and be seen more often.

A balance had to be struck between keeping faith with the loyal public and moving with the times.

With "Haw Haw" which had Max Miller, Ben Lyon and Bebe Daniels in the cast, it succeeded in continuing the Variety appeal and atmosphere.

Ben Lyon and Bebe Daniels had been working in England for two years and had become accustomed to English needs and styles, adding American innovations as seemed appropriate.

One "bit" which Ben Lyon worked in the show was not entirely original as it had been done in the USA by Milton Berle, where Lyon no doubt had seen it.

The idea was that Lyon started to sing, "A pretty girl is like a melody," only to be interrupted from the audience with the challenge, "Do you think you can sing that old song and make a success of it?"

Lyon rises to the bait. "I will bet you £5 that I can be a sensational hit. I can sing this song so well the audience will give me an incredible reception. It's all down to style and personality, not to mention good looks ....."

Edna Powell in "Haw Haw"

A young lady has entered (to a gasp of appreciation and expectant glances from the audience. She stands back up against the cloth out of Lyon's line of sight. He imagines that it is all for him. He thanks them for their enthusiasm. He is blithely unaware of Edna Powell's presence.

With a complacent and self-confident air, "Mr. Conductor, my music please." He starts. "A pretty girl is like a melody ...." and Miss Powell begins to disrobe, the garments fluttering in the spot.

Lyon pauses. He is basking in the warmth of the response." There you are. What did I tell you? They love it! It never fails! If you have the style and the ability."

He resumes. "She will leave you and then, come back again ...." Roars of appreciation and applause as further pieces of peach coloured flimsiness are discarded.

"A pretty girl is just like melody."

Miss Powell has some way to go.

"I told you," Lyon exclaims to the unseen heckler, "give me my £5." The roars of approval continue. Lyon looks at the audience. "Would you like an encore?"

Shrieks, roars, yells. "Yes! Yes! Encore!"

Edna Powell: "A Pretty Girl is like a melody", with Ben Lyon

"Do you really?" Disbelief - "want me to do an encore?"

Once again, "a pretty girl is like a melody ...."

A spot on the girl. She moves and reveals in time with the music. The crucial moment. A final turn coincides with the final notes of the song.

Blackout; off ad lib, "A pretty girl is just like a melody."

A memorable bit. Pace, polish, verve: Variety.

The Holborn Empire Orchestra, drawn by Feliks Topolksi

Gaston Palmer
"All ze spoons in all ze glasses"

Also appearing in "Haw, Haw" was the Juggler Gaston Palmer, styled "Anglo-French" who was always a delight to the Holborn's patrons whenever he played there.

Balancing billiard balls on a cue held on his chin and a top hat on a cane, balanced on a cane were bagatelle to him: surprising one might have thought for the personification of the bumbling stage French man.

But his tour de force was, in the words of his repeated patter, "All the spoons in all the glasses," a very difficult trick contrived to look difficult. Eight spoons in eight separate glasses, arranged in holders on a tray.

He was one of those who specialised in "missing" his tricks, but missing so often that in fact the act was all about missing, failing to get the spoons in the glasses. His air of

Gaston Palmer: "All ze spoons in all ze glasses"

desperation, the glasses and spoons teetering as he swayed, time after time, essaying the extremely difficult task, intoning his mantra again and again, willing himself, against all the evidence that all the spoons will go into the announced position.

"All ze spoons in all ze glasses." His crazy inaccuracies were performed against his own breathless, incredible, enthusiasm for his intended feat. His strivings for success soon engaged the sympathies of the audience and it was his custom to miss the trick up to 40 times, with a recorded of 55 at Holborn in this show.

Palmer reckoned to have practised this routine three hours a day a year, to get it right. Even allowing for a degree of publicity exaggeration in this it obviously took a lot of hard work. The act of confidence needed to delay the successful conclusion of the act may be imagined.

Gaston Palmer deserves a salute for pleasure given and as one of those speciality acts: Ganjou Brothers and Juanita; Wilson, Keppel and Betty; Bob Williams and Dog; Wences, among others who raised the genre to a new level.

Bebe Daniels brought her American experience to bear. She appeared in dance scenes with the Darmora Ballet, "The Dances of Yesteryear" with style and verve. In the Mexican number she wore the huge sombrero she adopted in the film "Rio Rita."

She had a fine selection of songs to sing, "I went to Havana;" "As round and round we go" and "Your company is requested." She formed a major part of the revue's success.

Also adding music and fun were Syd Seymour and his band, one of those so well remembered as top features of Variety in company with Dr. Crock and his Crackpots, Billy Cotton, Syd Millward and the Nitwits who all provided a large measure of comedy and fooling into their music.

This show added greatly to the lightening of London's spirits early in the War, as did

Gaston Palmer throwing the second billiard-ball onto the first.
Holborn Empire, June 1940

"Apple Sauce," a revue of similar type which was playing when German bombs put Holborn out of action for ever in 1941.

- ooOoo -

Labour Relations, Conditions of Employment and Totalitarian Regimes were problematical areas for variety performers, who by the individual nature of their work and offerings, largely dependent on personality, were sturdily individualistic and resented intrusion on their patch.

The problem was more acute with American acts because they frequently had film or record success behind them and made sure that they got full publicity. There had been protests from Musicians when Paul Specht's Band was playing here. In consequence Jack Hylton was forced to employ a balance of American musicians when he visited the States in 1936. The fact that Paul Specht's father was a United State's Senator may not have been unconnected with this decision.

American film star, Buddy Rogers, got great publicity out of a kidnap threat. "The Gangsters have followed me to London." Scotland Yard took the matter seriously. "The Daily Express" wondered if the threatening phone call might not have been a hoax.

Frequent visitors to this country were the close harmony singers, the Mills Brothers, who were always warmly received. Their restrained and melodic style being more suited to British tastes. Their records show that they never appeared to be trying too hard.

But also appearing at Holborn Empire in 1933 were Duke Ellington and his band. The "Era" critic did not care for the music on offer, but not surprisingly enjoyed "Mood Indigo." Perhaps the British Public were beginning to understand that Genius comes in many forms.

Gracie Fields, Max Miller (whom Joyce Grenfell records going to see, no doubt for lessons in timing), George Formby Jnr., Les Allen, Elsie Carlisle, were all frequently to be seen at Holborn as the Thirties progressed. Though Elsie Carlisle was criticised as "....sounding like an American when singing."

WEEKS IN VARIETY

Theatre Royal - Portsmouth 1954

When the Hippodrome, Portsmouth, was bombed in 1941, the town was left without a number one variety date; the Empire or Coliseum was a minor hall and the King's, Southsea, was increasingly playing touring musical comedies, plays or revues. The Royal was a repertory theatre almost opposite the Hippodrome, which remained as a cavity for many years, having been destroyed and demolished.

However, a change of policy put Portsmouth back on the Moss Tour and a lively presentation was generally available. This was certainly true in 1954, a late-flowering of successful theatre, where the business remained good, partly because of its ready accessibility near the central station, on all bus routes and not too far from the dockyards. In this respect, among others, it took over from the Hippodrome, where early in the war, with uncertainties prevailing, artistes could not be guaranteed a salary but were put on shares. But the Max Miller bill drew vast crowds, escaping from war threats, savouring the boy himself and the company got salary and a half. The business was usually there to be done.

In this declining year there were several very prominent bill-topping attractions: Tommy Trinder, with his own show; Peter Brough and Archie Andrews; the Beverley Sisters; Gary Miller; David Whitfield – all helped by those middle-of-the-bill turns which were actually the essence of variety. One of these, Joan Rhodes, "The Mighty Mannequin," was recorded a responsive welcome in this and other weeks.

Joan had presence. Dressed in an electric-blue, figure-hugging dress, which scintillated in the spot, she drew the eyes and attention of all. Two ladies sitting near me were moved to admiration of her shapeliness which, they were certain, owed nothing to artifice and a long slit in her skirt revealed an attractive leg. Her blonde hair shimmered.

To warm up she turned her attention to nails and steel bars which soon parted under her forceful twisting. Local telephone directories were soon demolished, lengthways and across; these feats achieved without loss of composure or ruffling of hair-style.

Her patter was effective, if conventional; an adjunct not a justification – huskily, "I can't help being powerful ..." She dragged willing men volunteers, clinging to a rope, across the stage.

"I have trouble with boy friends ... my last one asked for a squeeze and I broke his back." This all made for consummate variety; one's attention held, gaze riveted, ears open. Joan's appeal was, "You like me, don't you? I'm really rather beautiful, don't you think? (Actually I don't know if she was

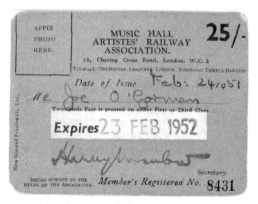

Membership Card of the Music Hall Artistes' Railway Association, 1951

beautiful or not.) Fancy such a strong girl being so attractive! Who dares to tangle with me?"

In an era when girls were conventional, unadventurous and placid, Joan broke the mould. She dared to be different and gloried in it. Accordingly, from Portsmouth to Bolton, to Edinburgh, to Dewsbury, Chiswick, Derby and Finsbury Park, for several years she walked her mannequin's cat-walk, the boards of Empires and Hippodromes before us, the entranced and delighted customers.

Also on this bill was Alan Clive, "A Host of Stars," an impressionist with polish, an interesting personality and one who threw light on the prevailing atmosphere of the time. For at that time many turns were attempting to be "American-smart" – whether that was an aim to be encouraged, or whether it helped the business is, perhaps, questionable. There are many who consider that Vaudeville in the U.S.A. went into decline in direct proportion to the number of performers who wore dinner jackets. The artiste's make-up was a fundamental part of his act and appeal; a recognisable trade-mark. But "authorities" came to decide that it was old hat and not smart to wear funny clothes, wear a fright-wig or have a grotesque hat.

Artistes were jealous of their individuality. The story is told one of rushing into the big dressing room at the Oxford, very pleased wit himself and saying, "I've just come from the Tivoli and Robey refused to follow me!" To which T.E. Dunville, a very caustically-witted man, replied, "I'm not surprised, you've got his make-up on!" That is with colourable imitations of the great man's hat, cane and frock-coat.

Around the same time there was a move to present "refined" variety, all shaded lights and potted palms. But many resented this as a threat to vitality and originality. So much so that, in one back-stage altercation between manager and comedian, the comedian's riposte was that Pike's Circuit (of cinemas) would soon take over the theatre anyway.

Membership Card of
The Vaudeville Golfing Society
for 1952

However, in the 1950's Alan Clive was polished, debonair suave even. He was going to give a finished performance and he certainly succeeded. His turn was compelling, smiling and gracious. Not, I suppose, remembered at all, he had presence and that indefinable something which makes a performer a bit special. I always felt that in the America of the 1930's, he would have moved into films and excelled in light comedy and light romantic roles. Anyway, he was entertaining and pleasing. His turn kept one looking at the stage and that sense of heightened expectation is the first, perhaps the only, essential for an act – to have drawing power and appeal.

Providing that grace and athletic vitality where circus and variety overlapped were the Six Flying De Pauls (is Lyndsey anything to do with them, I wonder?) whirlwind tumblers; with handsprings, flip-flaps, all in the most rapid succession, an all-girl act. Coldly analysed the act was nothing special from a technical point of view, but for exhilaration, eye-appeal and challenge it was a winner. The girls worked soundly and consistently in the latter days of variety and I hope they benefited greatly from their exertions. Thankfully, in the changed conventions of the halls, they did not go on last, the unenviable lot of acrobats since time immemorial. It was the top-of-the-bill who closed the proceedings in the latter days and certainly the Flying De Pauls deserved much more than to be the recipients of the traditional remark of ill will, "May all your children be acrobats!" (i.e. go on last, work hard and never earn any money).

It is pleasing that the New Theatre Royal has opened for business this year 1997. Everybody associated with this enterprise deserves every accolade for rescuing a theatre from the dark.

Hippodrome - Brighton - 1946

Many have written about the raffish charm of Brighton – London – on holiday by the sea. The excited visitors poured down from the Station, as described by Graham Greene, looking for fun, diversion, a good laugh and a blow-out.

The Hippodrome stood snugly in a side street, smugly perhaps, tucked away, but welcoming them all. Inside was a circle which proclaimed the Hippodrome's circus background – lightbulbs all round – but it always had a welcoming atmosphere, no draughty barn this. The most reluctant wife, taken against her will, by a husband who was determined to have an evening's entertainment in the theatre, would ultimately succumb to the light-heartedness, so typically Brighton and laugh as heartily as Rosie.

The stage door seemed determined to protect the performers, only a miniscule opening opening in a metal shutter-type door gave access back-stage and to the dressing rooms, one of which, highly prized, was at stage level, only a few feet away from the side. The remainder were upstairs.

Shows always went well there. The general air of relaxation no doubt freed performers from their anxieties – they were confident of a good reception.

One who radiated self-confidence was Renée Houston, appearing with her husband, Donald Stuart. No shrinking violet, her personality filled the building. Nobody could have been more suitable for the Hippodrome. Her Scots burr, at times more noticeable than others, her obvious beauty – perhaps a bit faded at this time, her red hair and piercing glance, all left an indelible impression.

I soon caught her attention. "I know who you are. Do you know me?" An impossible question for a ten-year old. "Mrs. Houston" I mumbled, hesitantly.

"*Mrs. Houston*," she chuckled, "hardly that but Mrs. anyway ... Where do you go to school?" and I told her. "Do they give you the stick?" I had to confess that they did – sometimes.

"In my school, in Glasgow, we used to be sent to the hardware shop with sixpence to buy a cane and bring it back to the school. I always used to drop it down the drain. Mind you, we used to get a double walloping for that. But I didn't care ..." All this with an inimitable grin, a character which radiated. If it took personality, style and wit, she had it and she took it on the stage, so it spread out from the boards and gathered everybody in. Donald was the perfect foil for her and she depended on him a great deal.

Oldham	details
Mrs. Duckworth, 14, Barugap Road	FB 1, D 1, OL, A 3
Mrs. Harding, 73, Greengate Street	WA 1, S 1, D 1, A 3
Mrs. Arthur, 72, Greengate Street	WA 1, C 1, A 2

Oxford	
Mrs. D. Day, 18, Beaumont Street	FB 3, BB, S 4, D 4, A 12
Mrs. J. Bateman, 80, Botley Road	FB 3, BBS, BB, S 1, D 2, A 5
Mrs. Singleton, 22, Castle Street	FB 3, BBS, S 1, D 2, NB, A 5
Mrs. Wade, " Montrose," Folly Bridge	FB 4, BBS, BB, S 3, D 2, A 7
Welsh Pony Hotel, Gloucester Green	FB 4, BB, D 5, S 4, A 14
Mrs. K. Tombs, 207, Iffley Road	FB 3, BBS, BB, S 2, D 1, A 4
Mrs. D. H. Barnes, 27, London Place, St. Clements	FB 3, S 2, D 2, NB, A 6
Mrs. W. Archer, 96, Morrell Avenue	BBS 2, BB, S 1, D 1, A 3
Mrs. Sanders, 10, Paradise Square	BBS 2, WA, D 1, NB, A 2
Miss E. Bushnell, 11, Paradise Square	FB 2, D 1, NB, A 2
Mrs. Sanders, 26, Paradise Square	WA 1, D 1, NB, OL, A 2

Perth	
Mrs. Masterson, 1, Albert Place. Tel. 815	FB 3, BBS, S 1, D 1, A 3

Peterborough	
Mrs. S. Simpson, 95, Dickens Street	FB 2, D 2, OL, A 5
Mrs. L. Ellis, 571, Lincoln Road	FB 3, WA, S 2, D 1, NB, OL, A 4
Mrs. Binns, 9, Towler Street	FB 2, BBS, BB, WA, S 1, D 1, NB, OL, A 3
Mrs. D. Wright, 25, Towler Street	FB 2, D 1, A 2
Mrs. G. Comber, " Camden," 58, Westbrook Park Road, Woodston	FB 3, BBS, BB, S 1, D 2, A 4

Plymouth	
Mrs. Russell, 11, Admirals Yard, Stonehouse	FB 2, BBS, BB, WA, S 3, D 3, NB, OL, A 6
Mrs. Claude Yelding, 32, Anstis St. (side door)	FB 3, BB, BBS, D 3, A 4
Mrs. J. Sandoe, 39, East Street, Stonehouse	FB 2, BBS, BB, WA, D 2, NB, OL, A 4
Mrs. R. Brown, 55, East Street, Stonehouse	WA 1, NA, S 1, D 1, OL, A 3
Mrs. C. Terrell, 13, Hobart Street, Stonehouse	FB 2, BB, WA, D 1, NB, OL, A 2

48

Plymouth continued	details
Mr P. Ayres, 2, Holyrood Place, The Hoe. Tel. Plymouth 61460	FB 2, WA, S 4, D 6, A 16
Mrs. A. E. Williams, 6, Holyrood Place, The Hoe	FB 3, BBS, BB, S 1, D 1, A 3
Mrs. E. Ford, 41, Kingsley Road. Tel. Plymouth 610091	FB 3, BBS, BB, S 2, D 1, A 4
Mrs. Higgins, 3, Melbourne Place	FB 2, S 2, D 2, NB, OL, A 6
Mrs. C. Buckler, " Bondi," 3, Morrish Park, Goosewell Road, Plymstock. Tel. Plymstock 3147	FB 3, BBS, BB, WA, NA, S 2, D 2, C 2, A 4
Mrs. Woodward, 13, St. James Terrace, The Hoe. Tel. Plymouth 61820	FB 3, BBS, BB, WA, NA, D 3, A 6
Mrs. V. Welch, 22, St. Lawrence Road, Motley Tel. Plymouth 5538	BB 1, S 2, D 1, A 3
Mrs. E. Morris, 39, Underlane, Plymstock, nr. Plymouth. Tel. Plymstock 2097	FB 2, BBS, BB, D 1, A 2
Mrs. M. Foster, 36, Union Place, Stonehouse	FB 2, D 1, NB, A 4
Mrs. Heckles, 93, Union Street	FB 2, A 8-10
Mrs. O. B. Bennett, 8, Windsor Street, The Hoe	FB 2, BBS, BB, WA, S 1, D 2, OL, A 5-6
Mrs. G. E. Clayton, 27, Wyndham Square. Tel. 606111	FB 3-5, BBS, BB, S 4, D 4, A 12

Pontypridd	
Mrs. F. M. Watkins, 82, Wood Road	FB 2, D 1, NB, OL, A 2

Portsmouth	
Mrs. Freebody, 5, Alexandra Road, Lake Road	BBS 2, DC 1, NB, A 2
Mrs. S. Banks, 134, Clive Road, Fratton	FB 3, BBS, BB, WA, NA, D 1, OL, A 2
Mr. G. Clinton, Alpine House, 562, Commercial Road. Tel. Portsmouth 73100	FB 4, BBS, BB, S 3, D 4, A 14
Mrs. M. Newton, 41, Locksway Road, Milton	FB 3, BB, D 1, A 2
Mrs. B. Fairfax, 75, Victoria Road North	FB 3, BBS, BB, WA, NA, S 3, D 6, A 12

Preston	
Mrs. V. Proctor, 16, Bairstow Street	FB 3, WA, D 4, A 8
Mrs. O. Walmsley, 42, Chaddock Street	FB 3, BBS, BB, D 3, C 3, A 8
Mrs. J. Lonsdale, 27, Frenchwood Street	FB 3, S 1, D 2, A 10
Mrs. L. Anderson, 44, Frenchwood Street	FB 2, BBS, BB, WA, NA, S 1, D 1, NB, OL, A 4
Mrs. D. Hinde, 36, Great Avenham Street	WA 1, D 2, A 4
Mrs. Cansfield, 38, Great Avenham Street	WA 1, NA, D 1, A 2
Mrs. M. Porter, 10, Latham Street	BB 2, WA, S 2, D 2, C 1, A 7
Mrs. L. Williams, 31, Lawson Street	FB 2, WA, S 1, D 2, OL, A 5

49

Some of the V.A.F. approved lodgings, 1951

She appeared with Charles Laughton in a West End play, "The Party" in 1957. Laughton's entrance was long delayed until, after much discussion about him and his character, he suddenly became visible in the shadows, listening all the while to the less than complimentary remarks about his personality and his disruptive and antisocial behaviour. All very effective, but the real impression, for me at least, was made by Renée in a character role. She, true to her variety training, made sure that all the audience heard every syllable of her lines. This was further proof of how variety performers could excel in the "legitimate" theatre if given the chance; a chance not often available in this country, as distinct from the United States where interchanges were not only possible but frequent.

Renée's late occupancy as the guiding light and anchor-person of "The Petticoat Line" ensured the success of that popular radio show. Always witty and resourceful, she kept the show on course and never allowed the irrelevancies or inconsequentialities of the other panellists to detract from the avowed and ultimate aim of the discussion.

Personality, grasp, flair, awareness, spontaneity were all Renée's. We remember her with affection.

Another attraction of Brighton was a remarkable example of theatrical digs to be found near the theatre at the end of the Street, a mere two minutes – genuinely – perfectly placed, called Ross Mansions. The proprietor, Mr. Ross himself, understood performers and their needs. His apartments were a veritable haven, especially as, at seaside places the night wind always seems to scud with a relentless persistence when the streets are bare. The performers were more than grateful to escape those forlorn pavements.

But I like seaside towns and Brighton's Hippodrome remained a constant factor in my affections.

Arthur Askey 1939-41
Palace Manchester

"Big Hearted" Arthur they called him. A more appropriate title could not have been found to satisfy the need Britain had to express itself as it stood up, geographically little, to the massed hordes on the Continent. The nation's cheeky self-confidence found a ready echo in the wisecracks of the diminutive man from Liverpool. Errand boy, coster, bus conductor ("Eye-thang-you") ready representatives of the irrepressible British type found from Gateshead to Goole were all embodied in Arthur's confounded smartness. "Bandwagon" had given him a national reputation and following after years of crackle and jingle. The catch-phrase ruled.

"Hello Playmates" toured the variety circuits in 1941 and the show's appearance at the Palace Manchester was part of a triumphal progress.

"There must be some bad films on this week" was Arthur's modest comment as he surveyed the holiday audience. Perhaps there was something in what he said though he was being unnecessarily disparaging. His solo turn worked just as well as his shadow on the air and, with all due respect to Dickie Murdoch, he could get on well without a foil. There was an infectious quality about his cheerfulness (that essential war-time requisite – "Britain can take it") that made the simplest buffoonery enjoyable and lent the touch of genius to his comic gestures.

Dave and Joe O'Gorman: "I gave her that"
(*Painted by Mollie Field*)

His early material was simplicity itself, deriving from his years of experience in concert party at Shanklin, for instance, and at countless Masonic evenings. It had the essential merit of being perfectly suited to broadcasting over the air - not requiring an audience. And, like all successful practitioners of the sound medium, Arthur was a superlative reader, making it sound natural and not being read.

> "Oh! What a glorious thing to be
> A happy grown-up busy, busy bee ...."

and leading on to sure-fire references to boy scouts' knees and parsons' noses. Slightly vulgar, not quite nice, but familiar and an easy cause of mirth. He was recognisable as a funny little man - quite daring doing what so many would like to do given the chance.

In these first years of the war, his fame and popularity were legendary. At the Prince of Wales Birmingham (sadly later on it was blitzed) in the pantomime "Jack and Jill" with Billy Bennett, Dave and Joe O'Gorman, Bert Brownbill and Cora Goffin, his success was incredible. The pantomime ran for 19½ weeks, despite the extremely inclement weather in the first year of war and Emile Littler tried to get the Theatre Royal and the Paramount Cinema to extend the run even further, but there were other commitments to honour in any case.

Clarkson Rose, also appearing in Birmingham that season, was heard to remark that if all the other comics in all the other pantomimes were put up in opposition to Arthur Askey, he would still draw the public. All the others would get were those unable to gain admission to him. And there was much more than a grain of truth in that anyway. The customers were under his spell and would not be denied. Two women were discussing their forthcoming visit to the theatre. A third woman enquired what they were going to see. "You know, the Askey thing, at the Whatsit."

Dave and Joe O'Gorman in their Comedy Vent. act

Being instantly recognisable, Arthur had only to enter a building for everybody to stand and stare. He went with other performers one Sunday, to have lunch at Stratford-on-Avon. Entering the hotel, he remarked that it was time to "tie on the nosebag." Uproarious guffaws greeted this sally. Clearly he could have got laughs out of a telephone directory at that time.

But he needed "bits" for pantomime and was, naturally, introduced into those which Dave and Joe had practised and perfected over their years in the business. The cod band, the balloon dance, the "100 pennies" entrance, "Have what you like for tuppence" and so on. He proved a willing conspirator in the fun and was always willing to perform the various gags, exactly as described and suggested, not seeking to "improve" them on his own account. Such shrewdness was to serve him in good stead. He knew a good thing when he saw it and was sensible enough to realise his inexperience in the pantomime medium. And, later on, when he was recognised as a top pantomime performer, he was always generous enough to acknowledge the debt he owed to Dave and Joe O'Gorman, who had shown him much and included him in their antics. But this was sound commonsense for a pantomime is a team effort. Combination and fellow feeling are essential for the whole thing too "gel." Some artistes have failed to understand this and have remained aloof, seeing the show as a vehicle for their 20 minute spot only.

Arthur learned that the most effective way to play Dame is as a man with skirts on, not as a female impersonator. A man dressed up retains the essential incongruity and opportunities for the burlesque – the disguise that anybody can see through being an essential part of the pantomime make-believe, after all the audience has to do something on its own behalf. So he became "Big hearted Martha" in successive Christmas annuals, but in the early years of the war at the top of his form and with radio novelty, no opposition could stand up to him.

Arthur Askey had many later successes on T.V., shows and films. But in point of impact - less, compared with his lustre in these early war years. A prodigious talent.

The patrons showed their appreciation in the traditional way and in kind too. It was very unusual for Arthur not to receive at least one bottle of whisky after performances in "Hello Playmates" and the "Jack and Jill" panto. This in wartime, when such luxury commodities were in "short supply" – not that humour, wit or entertainment were ever in scant supply from Arthur.

Empire Kingston - 1952

The rotation of dates round the various variety tours, Moss, Stoll, LTV and so on, seemed to decide that the booking for Kingston came up at the end of March, or beginning of April, just about the start of the Easter holidays from school. So quite often we were picked up and taken to the Empire prior to the journey home.

In the first week of April 1952 a strong bill was assembled: The Beverley Sisters, Johnson Clark (and Hodge) and Billy Thornburn; real variety here not overloaded or based in favour of any one particular style. I recall some bills which had three double acts on them. With the inevitable throat-cutting and competition that followed such a week was a disaster. But the authorities did not seem to learn. For instance, they frequently booked band-shows several weeks in succession and wondered why the public grew tired of the monotony! Part of this problem was that the managements frequently handed over the booking for particular weeks to agents or the band leaders themselves with the result that the agents put in, too frequently, those on their books, not allowing any new talent to develop. It was the same with bands, they were generally a good draw and the management were happy to pocket their fee without any responsibility.

It was suspected that some acts were "office acts", ie they paid more commission than the recognised 10% in order to secure bookings and frequent return dates. Many good turns felt they were not getting a chance but could not voice their dismay for the almost certain fear of alienating "the powers that be." When protest surfaced, managements and agents were united in stating that "all the acts with drawing power are working." It certainly had a restrictive effect on maintaining the vitality of new growth and the liveliness of competition. The same thing happened at the BBC, where for a long period certain acts only were booked, but that's another story.

However, at Kingston that week variety flourished. Two clever speciality acts with real polish and precision got things off to a good start when we returned to the theatre for second house after egg, bacon and chips at a nearby cafe. Dad, I suppose, had made do with a couple of ham sandwiches brought in by Johnnie Rogers, their stooge at this time.

Dad did his usual first spot: newspaper gags, cross-talk, followed by the Irish song "A short time ago an Irishman named Doherty . . .", a breathless tale of social junketings, following the election of Doherty as MP and written by Jim Thornton, a wayward and unreliable American comedian. He was also, interestingly and in quite another style, the author of the ever-popular "When you were sweet sixteen". What good songs Americans produce! I hope Jim Thornton's relatives are still getting the royalties - but more likely he sold the song for a pittance outright.

Their first half turn was followed by Bill Thorburn, a wonderful pianist and father of June Thorburn, tragically killed in an aircrash.

Just before Dad's second half appearance, I saw him talking to the stage manager and he then came over to me, standing hopefully in anonymity, and said "We're going through the pass-door,, follow me up to the box. You might care to be there while I'm doing the interrupting for the vent-act." Might I like to! Did Eddie Gray juggle clubs? Climbing the stairs we stood in the dark shadows until the signature music started and then Dad took a chair and sat right forward, perching over the stage. In the time-honoured manner he continued to applaud after Dave's entrance and at that moment a full spot hit the box, like a searchlight it seemed. I had never really appreciated their power of illumination before. It made the red and blue floods and floats very insignificant. It seemed to bare one's soul and I shrank into the dimmest recesses of the box, terrified lest I should be seen and either be thought part of the act and be demanded to contribute or to spoil the act in some way. One understood the loneliness of the performer, perched out, solitary and by nervous energy, dynamic personality, sheer charm or all three, convince the audience that this was the finest and most entertaining act ever to appear. To do so a few times is remarkable; to sustain it over the years of a career is a feat of the greatest magnitude. It has nothing to do with the ability to make your friends laugh at home or at a local concert.

But, sitting as far out of notice as possible, sheltering from that penetrating, vital light, it was an eye-opener to the comedian's timing, control of the voice and power to work on an audience. Interrupt too soon and the listener's attention is divided, pitch the voice too low and the joke loses its punch. The slight upward inflection at the end of a phrase, to

Dave and Joe O'Gorman

point the tag line, was beautifully demonstrated. All, it may be added, without the benefit of a microphone as fixed in the box at Victoria Palace, where Jimmy Nervo and Eddie Gray were posted to disrupt Crazy Gang sketches. Sitting nearby that evening I appreciated as never before the need for utterances to be of the right number of words for impact and humour.

On stage the ventriloquial doll is garishly dressed. The girl stooge would enter to "interview" Dave.

> "Excuse me, are you Dave O'Gorman?"
> "No, the one in the middle in Technicolour."
> "*Quiet* please."
> "The manager said I could sit down, stand up or walk about. I think I'll
> sit down. Of course, I could sit down over there."
> "Sit down, stand up, walk about, but KEEP QUIET please!"
> "I will – I think I'll sit down here."

Pause, the audience senses it's coming. Too soon and you destroy the expectation, too late and it falls flat.

> "But I *could* walk about if I wanted to."
> "Quiet *please*! You're interfering with me getting my living. This is my
> bread and butter."
> "What would you do for a plate of tripe?"

Timing perfect, stress faultless, intonation striking. His gimlet eyes and the quality of his retorts continually proclaimed him. It was a privilege to be allowed so close to participate in the activity and the involvement produced a glow, a warmth, of recognition that here was something special. The art which conceals art. It seemed easy, effortless, no problem. Sheer professionalism and the magic of it speaks to me over the years. Entranced I walked down the stairs and forgot to take notice of the Beverley Sisters (but I did two years later at Portsmouth Theatre Royal).

In any case we had to leave promptly to get down to Sussex. We were ferrying Dave to Eastergate, somewhat further on from where we lived. Leaving the theatre, we walked the short distance to the cattle market where easy car-parking was readily available. Dave was very uncommunicative. Passing a street lamp I noticed his lips were firmly clamped together which mystified me somewhat. It was only years later I realised he was trying to avoid sucking up the noxious vapours of the night and not inhale the certain infections considered to lurk in them. So does superstition, even ignorance, persist. But whatever moisture there was in the air seemed to help the car engine purr smoothly. Soon we passed the turning from the Kingston-by-pass through Chessington, when the street lamps ceased, the main beam snapped on and the journey had really begun.

The Metropolitan - Edgware Road - 1952

In a faintly unattractive area of London "The Met" stood for jollity and for escapism. It stood on the pavement's edge and overshadowed it. No gaudy display proclaimed it. When it was shut nobody could be mistaken. Was the advance box-office ever available?

But once you turned up at the appropriate time, a good show awaited you. It had its habitués and they knew what they wanted and came in down Harrow Road from Kilburn, Paddington and Marble Arch. The theatre was well placed on a busy thoroughfare, known and celebrated. Not for nothing was it chosen as the place alibi for PC Dixon's murder the "Blue Lamp," Tessie O'Shea's twelve minutes giving the villains time to be seen and get back from robbing the cinema, without anybody noticing their absence but remarking on their presence. If you look closely at the bills outside the theatre, whose names do you see? None other than Morecombe and Wise, just starting then!

Dave and Joe O'Gorman: "Can you do a little sum for me?"

Inside it was distinctly Victorian. The Variety Theatre aroma, dust, face powder, cigars, beer and orange peel seemed more powerful there than in any other hall I recall. It made few concessions to the *theatre*, this was a music-hall, unashamedly frank, people's fare, uncomplicated and direct.

Not like Finsbury Park which, in view of its position as Moss' Empires' top London date, took itself rather seriously – if one stopped to analyse such matters, which wasn't often, as getting in to see the show was a much more vital preoccupation.

If The Met was a bit raffish, nobody minded. Bills were assembled, it seemed, with design to give the patrons a good time. Mark you, one night there was an outbreak of fisticuffs in the Gallery which led to the straight man on the stage to exclaim, "If you're going to throw him over make sure you don't hit the musicians!" But normally it was the on-stage activities which provided the fun. On this week: Dr Crock and his Crackpots, Dawn White and her Glamazons, Iris Sadler and Bobbie Kimber held sway.

Bobbie Kimber "Sex of one and half a dozen of the other" provided an unusual approach, a ventriloquist in drag, so offering and individual twist on the provision of voice and characters to his doll "Augustus Peabody." In effect Kimber had to create two choice characters and maintain two illusions, giving a new point to the hallowed question "Who's working you then?" And Bobbie looked the part too. The patter and cross-talk between "Augustus", dressed as a sailor, was pointed and entertaining. The act was clever response to the need of variety comedians to present well-tried ideas in a novel way, putting a new frame around old pictures. And he certainly succeeded, for when he removed his wig at his curtain call, this onlooker at least, was surprised to see a man's head. He had sustained two illusions and deserves the credit for his creation.

Iris Sadler was also at The Met that week and while many a comedian could be or called himself "cheeky" here was a comedienne who really was like that, a genuinely funny woman but smart and wise and sharp. There was no pathos or underplaying or melancholy à la Suzette Tarri, but the direct appeal. Iris worked a cool astrological act "What the Stars Predict" with interruptions, a novel and pleasing variation. The inventiveness of performers in thinking up a new way of doing the gags was remarkable and a tribute to their individuality and cleverness. But the astrological framework went down well and with Iris Sadler one obtained and retained the impression that she was enjoying herself and, by implication, if you were not there must be something wrong with you. Oh yes, her grin was infectious and carried her off the stage to a storm of applause. Iris was one of the few women to play Dame in pantomime and made a great success of it. All in all she was a remarkable personality and her projected presence abolished, apparently, the orchestra pit and established her position as one of the foremost stand-up comediennes of her time.

Croydon Empire - 1942

It was known by the parents of my friend Richard Stewart, who was staying in Sussex while his father was posted to RAF Tangmere that we had "theatrical" connections. "Would a visit to the theatre be possible?" "It would? How splendid!"

Croydon always seemed a date accompanied by hustle and bustle. The streets were busy, the theatre was central. A good bill assembled, Jones and Thomas ("Men were deceivers ever"), Pat Stainer, Buck Warren and Chic ("Moonlight in Mexico"), a western act which had a long run, a deserved tribute to their professionalism and polish – white stetsons, heeled boots, ropes, stock whips and guitars; poise, polish and panache well in evidence. They had style. Chic told gags while spinning a rope. It was actually a three handed act – the girl was called Judy.

Buck Warren & Chic. A display from a 1937 edition of The Performer *advertising their return appearance at the Wintergarten, Berlin*

The chance to loiter at the side of the stage was eagerly welcomed. Buck Warren was to pass by. To a cowboy-infatuated lad this was, in anticipation, more exciting than the arrival of the Deadwood Stage. Sure enough, with a clicking of heels they came, Chic Cooper first, very smart and alert, the epitome of any Western dream, vitality oozed from him; Judy, who carried the props which were to be used in a sort of folding cloth laundry basket left on the side behind a flat. No sooner than my eyes feasted on this confection of spangles and lacy white buckskin than Buck himself strolled into view. Concentrating on the performance to come, he exchanged the merest glance at the stage manager and had no words for the other performers or stage hands dotted around.

I sidled up to him. Surely this manifestation of cowboy skill would vouchsafe a word or impart some secret of Western lore. Conscious of my presence he looked down, fiercely. He had a sharp face and an eagle eye. This look said, "What are you doing here?" and, to reinforce the stare, a positive unfriendly sentence for me. "Make sure you keep quiet while we're on!" What a cleavage between future and present persona. How could a cowboy be so ungracious? What he could not know was that I'd been back-stage as long as I could remember and knew the ropes, almost as well as he understood his lariats.

But the style and staging of this act – each component fitted together in a perfectly harmonious fashion, all designed to be very attractive to the eye and easy on the ear,

"Variety's most beautiful Western act" indeed. It was simplicity to forget him and gaze enraptured at the whirling white manilla. It was a perfect example of the term Variety Act. It was various in all its appeal and obviously a performance to delight. Buck Warren, Chic Cooper (and Judy) were good – and they knew it.

His rather truculent, unsmiling manner taught one many things; that he was a professional who took his work very seriously, that he was determined to please his public, that he was determined to keep his name on the booking lists without question and that there must always be a certain tension, a preparation for release of nervous energy, in those who appear before a public, which would be critical.

Though rather chastened I took good care to see his act a second time that evening. It grew in its impressiveness with a unfailing appeal.

Quite in contrast to this was another turn on the same bill, an acrobatic juggler working in tails. He did some bends and twists to a moderate reception, pranced a few unconvincing steps and finally balanced his top hat, by its rim, on the bridge of his nose. But from the side it was painfully plain that his balancing as assisted by a strong piece of elastic round the back of his neck, hidden by his ears. Oh dear! What a shattering of illusion. The topper was in no danger of falling off, no matter how fast he turned his somersaults. The poor follow was not fit to be on any stage, let alone share it with Buck and Chic. In any case his was an act which could have been seen in any town, at any hall, any week. Buck Warren's act was unique, if not in its idea, certainly in its inspiration.

All this excitement meant that Dave and Joe's performance occupied my attention less than usual. "If you were out in a rowing boat with your Mother and your sweetheart and the boat sank, which would you save?" and "Can you do a little sum for me?" passed their familiar way, not disregarded, but this week at least, firmly in second place to the make-believe Wild West.

Plymouth - 1939

There is no atmosphere like the theatre's and the most compelling is in variety halls. Not merely inside the building but in the process which accompanied it, in preparation, in travelling, in living the experience for the week.

Plymouth, in the first days of the War, had its own aura. The life of the great naval port achieved a vitality and intensity derived from the frantic need to protect the convoys, hunt submarines, harry the enemy and engage him wherever he was to be found.

The town was full; lots of soldiers and airmen, mobilised, training, in transit. But it was the sailors who caught the eye. Caps, bell-bottoms, white gaiters for the shore-patrol. And a very real distinction between rolling Jack Stoker and upright hostilities-only ratings. To this haven we came, father and son, for the Palace re-opened after the closure of all places of entertainment. Eagerly awaited by the hordes who clamoured for entertainment and diversion and had booked a fine bill: Troise and his Mandoliers, Pim's Navy, their billing attracted

The V.A.F. date book

"Round the Halls": Dave and Joe O'Gorman's engagements for 1942

from every hoarding "The Bouncing Sailors" – how appropriate. They flung themselves at the poles on the edge of their spring mattress. "Round the corner!" Immediately answered by "I'll have a go at that!" and followed by a manoeuvre of the clumsiest ineptitude. Here was art to conceal art and a warming of the heart for the plucky, likeable, naive, fall-guy, unendingly optimistic with his readiness to have a go and find the surest source of sympathy-inspired laughter.

And then, eyes aching with the need for juvenile sleep, through, the blacked out streets to the hotel, high up on the Hoe. Through the rain which fell impalpable sheets. west Country seaside rain, competing with the other element for the mastery of the land.

Next morning to breakfast in the dining room. Porridge and kippers to a mixed clientele, naval blue and gold rings much in evidence, served by stately waiters who proffered, gravely, the complimentary small packet of De Reszke cigarettes, no use to us, but helpful to take home. The incipiently precocious theatrical demon provides an easy familiarity in conversational affability with all sorts and conditions, particularly if they show any sort of friendly demeanour or interest in a small boy.

A naval officer who was seated at a nearby table: "Good morning, Sir! I've got a clean shirt on. Have you got a clean shirt on?" This with a direct gaze at his immaculate uniform stiff collar, followed by his stifled laugh and straightforward answer, "Why, yes I have – we'll have to keep them clean won't we?" Every time I put a white shirt on I think of him with affection. Did he survive his dreadful duties and patrols, bitter weather, torpedo, mine and bomb? He's part of my Plymouth panorama.

Facing the rain was not to be delayed but it could only be dealt with by wearing the proper gear, duly bought, a yellow oil-skin sou'wester, from which the water cascaded in permanent rivulets, leaving its occupant dry and safe, on our retraced steps to the Hoe where the lighthouse stood, its basic stance proclaiming solidity to the world. And we climbed, step upon step to the viewing platform, imagine inside, going round and round and up and up to the top. What memories conveyed to the theatre with its palpable heady aroma, dust burned by the limes, make-up and the pungency of uncle's cigars.

In the late evening routine, twice-nightly, and tingling excitement standing at the side of the stage wreaked havoc with patterns of sleep, which did not come easily after so much visual and musical stimulation. The urge to play the "bouncing sailors" – the so-called "Boundary Act" from bed to bed drove thoughts of rest far from awareness. But the debt of sleep like all accounts had to be paid and the afternoon remedy was the cinema. Gary Cooper in "Beau Geste" – once seen never forgotten and on several afternoons the warmth and accumulated tiredness brought sleep until, protesting, it was time for the theatre again.

"And now we have 'Troise and his Mandoliers' ", a splash of colour; yellow, red, green and lilting syncopation of the massed instruments. Catchy, unusual and Pascale sold his act beautifully, with verve and style. You *had* to enjoy it, no question it *was fun*. Twice nightly, with popular appeal and a stage hint of some sunlit land across the sea where the sun always shines and war is but a word. So many "Workers' Playtimes" and "Music While You Work" spread this charm to many a gloomy spot and redeemed the monotony of a war-time factory bench and AA gun-site. But alive in the theatre was his special glory – the Mandoliers filled the stage like a sunrise.

There was no sunrise outside the theatre in Plymouth that week. The rain took on a malevolent characteristic changing its nature by the hour, but ever-threatening with moisture that attacked in an infinite variety of forms impelled by a wind that drove across the Sound, raising white waves and emphasising the forlorn aspect of the coast.

House-by-house, Dave and Joe worked their own transformation; changing the nature of Dr Jekyll and Mr Hyde, in a way quite unforeseen by the eminent writer of that singular tale.

By the baleful light of a green lime, Dave with recourse to a small table covered in coloured bottles, contrived the impression of altering his personality along and in harmony with his appearance. Ribald interruptions from the front accompanied his burlesque acting, a parody of the well-known cinema portrayals.

"Graargh! Aargh!" as he drank the potion draining it to the dregs.

"What an actor!"

"There's a gentleman to see you Sir. He calls himself Frankenstein!"

The flickering of the lime and the livid transformation produced a macabre and truly hilarious response.

"I see you've got your new set in!"

Another menacing glare and scowl, a horrendous change of state.

"Bring him his Bob Martins".

A Victoria Palace programme of 1925

The essentially ridiculous nature of the change soon became apparent to me, so young, in the hearty response of the patrons and the absurd posturing on stage.

Soon it was time to pack and prepare for our departure, which would be I was assured by the night train, direct to Sussex, another prospect to savour in tingling anticipation, a steam train at night. And still it rained with a furious gale and we found ourselves trudging gamely with our bags to the station through the black streets, deserted, mysterious, awash with no light visible. My plea "Got your torch Joe?" was a cry for reassurance on two counts; that we would reach the station, impossibly far away, and to know that he was there and would find the way.

Casino, W1 - 1947

It was the Christmas holidays from school and pantomime this year was to be at the London Casino, for Emile Littler – "Mother Goose." But this was not in our thoughts as we journeyed by train on the first day. The prospect of spending time in London preparatory to returning to Slindon was exhilarating: shops, presents, cinemas, visits, were matters of more importance.

Snow had fallen early that year, deadening the sound of vehicles and footsteps as the cavalcade proceeded to empty the school for its Christmas breather. Sharp frost sealed the flakes so the suburban landscape, glimpsed from the speeding train, took on an entranced quality – could there have ever been a more ideal start to the Yuletide festivities?

Reliable as ever, Dad was at the Waterloo barrier, smiling, reassuring and knowing that he too was participating with more than ordinary enthusiasm. He knew what boys home from school wanted and looked forward to. "Well son, we have to get to the theatre for rehearsal this afternoon but first I thought a visit to Hamleys would be the thing." Hamleys! Soldiers! and so it proved after a taxi-ride over the river to find us on the milling pavement, in a crowd who obviously had similar enterprises on their mind. Mounting the stairs to the floor displaying the lead models, so beloved, father and son both experienced a flurry of expectation because it was known that new varieties were in stock, a wider range than war-time stringencies had allowed, when they were available, which for several years was not at all.

And there, vividly apparent among the khaki tommy-gunners, helmeted sentries, rigid grenade-throwers, sappers,

Iris Sadler

miners and riflemen were the new species. Peacetime creations, new, never seen before! They were solid in construction and in appearance. Duke of Wellington's Guardsmen looked out like the Iron Duke himself. Tunic, knapsack, musket and shako so firm and bold; the detail of frogging and sabretache exact and neat 18th century grenadiers were resplendent in coats of startling red with yellow facings and white knee-breeches, their accoutrements and tricorne hats proclaimed them. Their officers struck an easy languid pace, apparently manipulating their canes with a studied elegance. The tricorne hats perched with a nonchalant grace and these, 12 of each, were to be mine! And, joy of joys, some for my brother too.

So we entered the theatre for the rehearsal. It seemed different to others I had known: a bit more formal, serious, earnest even – very conscious of being W1. Dad had filled me in on the people appearing: Stanley Holloway, Nat Mills and Bobbie, Celia Lipton and that excellent stand-by Con Kenna (and Pilot), "The Flying Fools." But the attitudes and demeanours of the performers on the stage seemed as familiar as ever. We sat at the side of the stage, on a prop log, our backs against a flat. The stage was rehearsal lit and all a bit low key. The rehearsal involved the chorus, a large one, and the Fairy Queen's first entrance. She appeared from behind a cloth, her wand upraised. Dad chuckled quietly, "First Fairy Queen you've ever seen with her slacks on!"

Uncle Dave appeared and they walked through their chorus outside the "Horse and Hiccup" and were finished for the day and we left and spent the next hour or so in the Newsreel cinema at the bottom of Shaftesbury Avenue. The liveliest cartoon was "Christmas Comes But Once A Year", which featured a cartoon of a train, designed to deliver presents and other goodies all round the house, with hilarious consequences as the engine doubled as a teapot.

Iris Sadler and Company in Francis Laidler's "Aladdin"

So back to the flat with the prospect of more thrills on the morrow; And the first of these was breakfast at Lyons Corner House, Marble Arch. Never had bacon smelled so appetising or toast so appealing. We were very early I recall – very few people were taking early breakfasts but the rehearsal call was an early one: the show needed knocking into shape. This time I was given a bit more freedom and wandered round the theatre from under the stage to fly floor. Nobody seemed to mind, they were all occupied with the full orchestra and lighting cues.

Before lunch we had to call on Emile Littler himself and I was carefully told to be sure to say "Meet the boys from Hanley" an absolute rigmarole to me. It was only some years afterwards that I understood where the heavy duty sanitary-ware porcelain glaze was manufactured and we had just paid a visit to what the Americans call "a comfort station!" It got a good laugh from the impressario anyway.

So to the afternoon train from Victoria across the snowy countryside to Sussex, precious soldiers in their boxes with the assurance that we would all see the pantomime in a week or so.

And we did, as part of a packed house revelling in the Baron (Stanley Holloway) ordering the witch away from his village, sympathising with Mother Goose, ugly, wondering at her transformation and criticising her for her vanity and pretence when the untold riches go to her head and shrieking, along with some grown men – heads of families, in response to Cup and Saucer's remarks to the witch.

"We don't know where you've hidden it but *we shall* find it!" – the elusive Golden Egg. Nat Mills was a convincing Dame, with Bobby, a memorable part of this show, as always.

Naturally there was a ballet; a very artistic and sensitive performance no doubt, in its own way, but my brother and I and the rest of the audience seemed united in uproarious enjoyment of the puncturing of the pretension in the balloon dance. The burlesque classical posing, in slow time, with the truly huge red globes being propelled slowly, to and from, to the strains of "Humoresque" by Dave and Joe with such serious and concentrated expressions on their faces was a masterpiece of silent humour, playing with the audience's response. The blue tunics worn by the brothers, their bony knees, Joe's red wig, worn back to front, all proclaimed this a pantomime high piece, a classic understanding of the medium The world of make-believe proved more real yet again than the world of artefact. The amalgam of enchantment in this "Mother Goose" was so strong as to make the most perfect model soldiers forgotten. Given the option, put to a vote, the visits to the Casino would have won hands down.

And during the interval Emile Littler passed by, smiling a little smile. No doubt he deserved to be complacent and satisfied but, of course, he had also seen the box-office returns.

- oo0oo -

Tumblers and Acrobats

These speciality acts made an easy transition from circus to Variety and formed an essential part of any bill – largely unremarked and certainly underpaid. Acquiring the skills was hard and constant practice. One household had a parrot which repeated all day "Come along, you boys. Get on with your practice!"

The hardest task-master was Papa Cragg. The threat to send recalcitrant juveniles to him for instruction was more than enough to produce a sustained flurry of bending, loosening-up and hand-springs. A notable teacher was Carlo Barello (Barello and Millay), a bar performer. His accolade "Joe's flip-flaps *is* good today" satisfied many a juvenile heart.

Such performers always took an element of danger with them. Most tragic was the performer killed at the Olympia, Dublin, who let go of the trapeze bar to fly to his catcher at precisely the moment when all the lights fused. His flight ended against the brick wall at the side.

Knockabouts could put extreme vigour into their work. McCabe and McNally performed so enthusiastically to make a hit that on the morning after their first appearance in New York, they had to help each other down the hotel stairs, nursing their deep bruises and strains. Pace, verve and style and a novel way of presenting a routine were always being sought. Conversation was frequently "Can you do a three-high?" "Yes I play a mandolin." The Whirlwind Elwardos, Freddy and Partner were particularly attractive modern turns in this genre.

Maurice Colleano could do a forward somersault under a table. The controller of a large chain of theatres felt that Maurice's words of explanation to the audience, to build the turn up, were merely slowing the act down and told him to cut them out. Realising that without the build-up much of the impact would be lost, Maurice cut the trick out completely.

The common theatrical curse "May all your children be acrobats" reveals the harsh realities of a tumbler's life: to go on first or last and never make much money. Indeed, it was only late in Variety's history that the Top of the Bill went on last, rather than the athletes who frequently performed to the audience's departure.

- oo0oo -

Minstrel Shows

The great Victorian and Edwardian popularity of Minstrel Shows was due, in large measure, to their supposed superior tone and lack of offensiveness; no women appeared in them. This allowed Royalty to patronise the troupes. The prejudice against females on stage, singing and dancing, did not die out with Nell Gwynn.

The Minstrel Show format encouraged the growth of cross-talk between Mr Bones, Mr Interlocutor and Mr Tambo, interspersed with choruses, songs and dances. No doubt the style and presentation grew tedious. Typical arguments about production were used in the film "The Jolson Story" with Jolson trying to branch out in an individual style A single turn could get more money in any case and be able to show off all his talents rather than as part of a production. It was a veritable hot-bed of talent and an invaluable training ground for double acts and turns.

An original American act was Coakley, Hanly and Donleavy who performed a miniature minstrel show – the three going through the range of techniques in a lightning turn. They would sit on three chairs, widely spread in one and advance and retire with trios (song and dance), end-men gags, single songs, dances and duets and finish with a tambourine finale, the pit orchestra playing *fortissimo*. A renewal of this idea was put up to the BBC in the 1950s but nothing came of it. They were hatching "The Black and White Minstrels" just then!

There was only one way to remove burnt cork: to strip off completely and make copious use of water and sponge. For convenience these pails were lined up against the back wall of the stage. While the Minstrels of the Howard Atheneum show were busily engaged bending over to complete their task, the drape hiding them from the audience fell silently from the flies. The ensuing roar prompted one performer to turn to his companion and remark, "Say somebody's making a hell of a hit out there!"

Lips were never made up by old time minstrels merely deeply pursed and turned inwards, leaving a satisfying pink-white mouth area.

THE PANTOMIME COAT

A recurring event was the appearance, about the middle of November, of the overcoat. A garment which proclaimed solidity, stability and substance and its emergence announced the start of the pantomime season, to be spent in a large, usually northern town, where the climate could be, especially in those smoke charged atmospheres, unfriendly with frost, snow and freezing fog. But the coat, blue, heavy, crombie made its own statement that here was the start of an important enterprise - for public and performer alike.

Actually the appearance of the coat was the culmination of events marking the process of signing the contract, being measured for costumes, attending the script conference and discussing any props, that would have to be made in the pantomime workshop. There were also arrangements to be made about all those extraneous but essential features so necessary for the pantomime performer. Wigs to be set and dressed for example, their crimped formality typically expected for the Dame in her various apparels. The dinner jacket for the pantomime ball and other formal affairs usually needed some thorough valeting and where were the silk black socks and braces?

The arrangement for forwarding pantomime kit from the store had to be put in had. The cow-cloth, song sheet ("Let's All Sing Like the Birdies" or "I Love To Hear The Band Play Pom Pom Pom"), the instruments for the band, including bass drum on which Hilter's face probably needed redoing, all needed checking. Shoes, photos, wig-stands, towels, dust-covers for clothes, the dummy for the dummy dance and the other assorted paraphernalia needed for playing a part and sustaining a, hopefully, long run.

One critical item for Dave and Joe was to procure a supply of balloons for their unique and idiosyncratic balloon dance. As the War entered its fourth year, for instance, this item was proving a real headache. The red and blue globes, three feet in diameter, always liable to burst or perish, had lasted out the previous year sustained by an extensive patchwork of elastoplast covered in lipstick. They were not going to hold out much longer and requests at toy shops only evinced the dreaded and frustrating response, "They're in short supply" – that is *none*. However, fortune favours the persistent and a chance visit to a tiny mixed shop, tobacco, groceries, some toys in Fulham produced results. "Oh yes Sir, I've lots of those. Put a stock in hand for the Coronation (1937) but they never sold well." "How many

Pantomime at Manchester Hippodrome, 1945

have you got?", not wanting to sound too eager. "Well, there seems to be six boxes here, a dozen a box." And irrespective of cost, all seventy two were rapidly purchased and the crucial property avidly acquired with a consequent loss of anxiety for that and future years.

Collecting and despatching luggage was the task of whoever had been engaged as "Stooge" for that season, either the diminutive Norman McGlen or Big Fred or latterly George Robertson or Johnny Rogers. All these unsung heroes made a distinctive contribution to the all round sufficiency and success of the pantomime and Big Fred made a wonderful sledge, at Birmingham, for us I remember. Fixing accommodation was an essential, early necessity. To ensure smooth relaxation and total concentration in the early days of the run it was customary to book a hotel for the first fortnight or so (this took care of Christmas arrangements, unless distance home made travel possible) and, having avoided the dreaded loss-of-voice, consequent on long use in playing parts as opposed to doing an act, the change into digs was a conventional move once the run was established.

"Babes" at Dudley Hippodrome, 1953

As Christmas drew nearer so the pace grew quicker. The difficulty of organisation for a long run in a fixed location was complicated by the weeks worked in Variety in the autumn, correspondence needing to be forwarded and producers to be contacted. One eagerly awaited letter was notification of the advance. One received speaks volumes for the high level of intensity in preparation for success that a first-class pantomime entailed. "I thought you might like to know about the advance. I don't know whether it is your name, my name, past successes or the weather but it is a fact: the evenings are simply wonderful and I am very pleased about it." This was from Emile Littler.

A cloud on the horizon perhaps to be dispersed, perhaps not, was the final confirmation of the other actors in the cast. Generally, the cast was steady from year to year. The same production would be transferred from centre to centre but there were usually changes, some major, some minor. A change of principal boy could be disastrous, some of them being too eager to convey the impression they were slumming, to the detriment of the show's effectiveness and the morale of others in the cast. "How *appalling* it would be to do this all the time," said one.

Booking the speciality act was crucial. One that could be introduced beneficially into the running of the performance and plot were infinitely preferable to one merely a fill-in before the finale. Wilson Keppel and Betty were ideal as "entertainment" before the

Emperor of China, Duke of Morocco or Vizier in the "Forty Thieves". Rather like the coat, an essential ingredient, not noticed till absent. And if the apparel oft proclaims the man, this coat stated his occupation and life too. Long live King Pantomime!

Chorus Song

Let's all sing like the birdies sing,
Tweet, tweet, tweet, tweet.
Let's all sing like the birdies sing,
Tweet, tweet, tweet, tweet.
Let's all warble like nightingales,
Give your voice a treat.
Take a tip from the birds,
Now your all know the words,
Tweet, tweet, tweet, tweet.

(Bill Wise)

Con Kenna with his "Flying" act

The Harris Twins (Sonia and Sylvia) in "Babes in the Wood" pantomime, Manchester, 1945-46 season

LYCEUM PANTOMIME

The reopening of a theatre dark for so many years is an event to be celebrated with a roll of drums and a fanfare of trumpets. Especially so in the case of the Lyceum, for so long the home of melodrama and, under the direction of the Melville Brothers, the true home of pantomime in London.

The shows were graced by lively principal boys, Jill Esmond, Nancy Frazer, Marjorie Sandford and beautiful principal girls, Ann Leslie and such talented dancers as Wendy Toye. The comedy was in the hands of such robust comics as Naughton and Gold, Eddie Gray, Dick Tubb, Clarkson Rose, the O'Gorman Brothers and Albert Burdon. One earlier pair of comedians rather presumed on their permanence (Mr Fred used to say to comedians who had made their mark, "You can come back here as often as you like. No more money though.") by waiting for the Melvilles at the crossing to Simpson's in the Strand and getting an invitation to lunch. Their contract was not renewed.

An Arthur Ferrier cartoon of the Lyceum Pantomime, 1937-38

There were also effective villains, Robert Bottomly ("Best Witches for Christmas"), Noel Carey "Uriah Creep" and pleasing speciality acts such as Newman, Wheeler and Yvonne, Pim's Navy "The Bouncing Sailors," and Latasha and Lawrence. The Melvilles' pantomimes were exuberant, colourful, lots of red and yellow in the sets, tuneful and above all fun. James Agate said they ran on a well tried formula. First the story, then the ballet and finally the comedians after, it must be said, a very long interval in which teas, orangeade and ice-creams were sold, all Melvilles' own brand, to the overheated audience.

The Brothers were an eccentric pair. It was their custom to buy up any old job lots of scenery or indeed anything that might be useful on day. Consequently the wrought iron railings, so decorative for St Paul's churchyard in "Dick Whittington" did equal service surrounding the palace in "The Queen of Hearts." These contradictions did not seem to matter. One particularly impressive purchase was a red London bus which driven onto the stage by one of the comedians allowed them to do their newspaper gags sitting on the step while having a break in their journey to find the Magic Sixpence. The Brothers loved to call a meeting to discuss the production. For these meetings they would put on bowler hats and brown dustcoats and were not above an ironic rider, "We want all the comedians to be there and you can come too Clarkie" and he, failing to see the joke, declined to attend.

After the run had settled down the Melvilles would make alterations to save money, "No more overtime. We know where all the big laughs are now, so that song of yours Clarkie – it will have to come out" and despite his expostulations, out it duly went. Wise the artiste who preferred to work in a front cloth.

The Melvilles had a keen appreciation of what the theatre and the public would take and in consequence always took the pantomime off when it had made £30,000. The popularity of the shows was immense and it was said that newly born children in the south east of London would be patted on the head and told "You'll be going to the Lyceum pantomime." Many a father at Christmas-time dug deep into his pocket to give his family the treat.

"Queen of Hearts" at the Lyceum Theatre, London. Produced 26 December, 1938

The pantomimes were often graced by the two Princesses Elizabeth, now Her Majesty, and Margaret Rose together with their mother, now the Queen Mother, who would watch the show from a box. The family would arrive without any fuss and after the lights had gone down His Majesty the King would arrive in an Austin Seven with his detective and enter unobtrusively by a side door and sit at the back of the box out of sight of the audience. The Princesses particularly enjoyed plate smashing and slosh routines.

Fred Melville's death just before the 1938-39 production "Queen of Hearts" enabled Bert Hammond who took over to make one or two much needed improvements and modernisations. An up-to-date jazz band was put in the pit and those rather elderly ladies of the chorus who had prompted Eddie Gray to say, "This is the bit I like, when the Grandmas come on" were replaced by more youthful dancers.

The Lyceum was a landmark. How fortunate that the theatre survived a road widening scheme to Covent Garden and German bombs, to reopen in such splendour. The spell is broken – on with the Play!

PETER FANNAN

An actor's life for me

Research aims to reveal or make plain things which were obscure or unknown or reveal a new aspect of a subject. These were more or less considered objectives when I set out to plan a talk for the British Music Hall Society's research group on Peter Fannan, comedian, primarily known for his clerical impersonations. Whilst engaged on this task, scratching about with it, I was surprised to receive a phone call with a query. "Was it correct that my father's sister, Norah, had married Peter Fannan?" I confirmed this and another question followed. Did the name Vicky Cornettie mean anything to me? I confessed that it did not. The following evening my phone rang again. This time the enquiry was whether Fannan was his proper name. In fact his name was McCormack. The search for Peter Fannan had been proceeding on two fronts. My caller told me that his wife, Gwynneth, was Peter Fannan's daughter, which was news to me as the name was not one given to the two daughters who were known to the family. Peter

Peter Fannan

Fannan (McCormack) was born on 18th November 1899, son of Rosa (nee Abbot) and Peter Fannan (McCormack) Snr of the well known act Foreman and Fannan ("Percy and Harold").

They were one of several acts of a style very popular in the Edwardian era, the broken down swell, tramps who have seen better days, the shabby genteel. Acts in this sort were Morny Cash "I live in Trafalgar Square," Ella Shields as "Burlington Bertie," the Brothers Harrison who sang:

> "We live on the Thames Embankment,
> Two students are we.
> We're always studying for the bar,
> Whenever we've got the 2d (tuppence – old
>   money – for a pint of beer).
> You've heard of the judge in the Law Court,
> There's only a difference slight –
> The judges they sit on the bench all day,
> We're on the bench all night."

And Ward and Vokes "The Millionaires" whose song "When You're on Broadway" was the opening chorus for so many seaside shows and in the USA Duffy and

Vickie Cornettie

Forman and Fannan

Sweeney and Charles "Tramp" McNally. There were many more and the type reached its full flowering in Charlie Chaplin who adopted George Robey's hat and cane, George French's tiny moustache and Fred Kitchen's boots and trousers, and put it all together into his memorable Little Tramp with the emphasis on the visual. Plus, of course, Fred Astaire and Judy Garland "We're a Couple of Swells." Foreman and Fannan adopted a drawling repartee: "I say H... H... Harold." "Yes, P... P... Percy" and had a solid following as worthy exemplars of the type, summed up in the thought "You might be like it yourself one day, one of the shabby genteel"

Peter Fannan, "The (E)Rector of Laughs"

Young Peter Fannan, as was the custom, followed his father into the business and developed an act as a comic clergyman, an enduring staple of British humour from Feste's satirical questioning of Malvolio, Marlow's guying of the Papacy in "Dr Faustus" to Jane Austin's oleaginous clergymen. In Variety, Vivian Foster created the apotheosis of the convention, "Yes, I think so . . ."

Peter Fannan obviously developed well. The illustration shows him confidently poised, a well tailored suit, the boater hat well off the face to reveal all nuances of facial gesture. He gave full effect to his opening song (with words in their original meaning), "I'm a giddy, little gay, young curate . . ." before launching his patter with "As this is the third Sunday after Pontefract . . ."

Tom Williams, celebrated Welsh baritone, and "Little Vickie", 1914

It is at this point that the story returns to Vicky Cornettie or Little Vickie as she was known at first, presumably on account of her youthfulness. The date on the back of the photo is 1914. Later she appeared as the Cornettie Trio with the "World's Renowned Welsh Baritone – Tom Williams." They worked all over the country on the top circuits. For instance, in May 1917 they worked at New Cross Empire, part of a bill with the revue "Nights of Gladness." The act continued until 1922 when Vickie and Peter Fannan's daughter was born. Vickie worked solo after this. How long Peter Fannan and Vickie were together is uncertain but in the same year Peter married Norah. After some time Peter and Norah were estranged. Whether the previous association with Vickie had anything to do with it is hard to say. Theatrical emotions and temperaments are notoriously fickle at the best of times.

However, by Christmas 1934 Peter and Norah were reunited and Peter had completed a busy and successful year's work, a ten month's run as principal comedian with "The Show's The Thing" and pantomime for Baldrick and Williams at Shepherd's Bush and Hackney Empires to follow. Not unnaturally Peter played Dame and he later branched out from his clerical routines to work in skirts in his usual Variety offering. At other times he portrayed his cleric in a hiking role, country walking being a very popular activity at the period and easy to guy: shorts for men and women being considered outré, even more so for a parson.

Booked by Reeves and Lamport, Peter continued to work regularly at good venues for the top circuits, Holborn, Finsbury Park in 1935 and the Pavilion Liverpool on 8th August 1938, Lewisham on 10th October 1938 and the Empire, Croydon on 12th December 1938. It seemed as if he had found a lasting and secure pattern of career and life, especially when a son, also called Peter, was born. However, Norah only lived a year after this and passed away in August 1939. Difficulties and war clouds came to create peculiar stresses. Young Peter was travelling with the act and with the non-availability of digs and cancellation of trains, father and son seem to have spent some nights sleeping under the stages of various theatres, the only refuge in times of severe blitz. Nothing daunted, Peter soon teamed up with Joan in the act Peter and Joan Fannan as a pair of flower sellers. There seems to have been a strong element of pathos in their work. They were working at the Empire, Nottingham on 1st June 1942, Finsbury Park on 25th January 1944, Scunthorpe on 20th February 1945 and the Coliseum, Portsmouth on 19th June 1945 – a healthy and solid spread. But Peter's health seems never to have been strong and he had a tendency towards hypochondria and July 1947 he suffered a stroke which left him paralysed on the right side. He eventually died in St Mary Abbots Hospital on 29th July 1949. His address was recorded as 21 Montpelier Square, Westminster. He was not yet 50 years old.

Peter and Joan Fannan, during their act at Collins' Music Hall, London

Vicki Cornettie lived on until 1990. Her passing stirred memories of events which had lain unspoken for many years. Among her possessions was an album of a type commonly kept by performers, who frequently kept collections of photos and autographs, sometimes both, as records of weeks worked, people met and friendships made. It was also an indication, albeit a fairly tenuous one, of the progress you were making. Vickie's album is a veritable treasure chest of photos with autographed good wishes from Variety people, with dates and places itemised to plot her date book. The preservation of Vicki's book is something to be thankful for.

In 1917, Ella Shields, Billy Merson, Cruikshank, Carlton, Daisy Dormer, Florrie Forde, Mona Vivian, Tucker, Wilkie Bard, Geo Mozart, Hetty King, Rastus and Banks, Harry Lauder, G. H. Elliott and Fred Barnes all signed her book, a Roll of Honour of the Business, at a range of venues from Finsbury Park, New Cross and Stratford to the Empire Harrogate and the Hippodrome, Middlesbrough.

The entries express friendship and esteem for her as a performer. Vickie was evidently a well-thought of act, at a time when musical playing skill and a singing voice with its own power were appreciated as desirable, praiseworthy and, indeed, marketable accomplishments.

In pre-microphone days voice and instrument had to get across; a cutting edge to son or instrument was essential. The same applied to makers of records on disc or cylinder.

Jack Smith, "The Whispering Baritone" was put on at the Coliseum and his voice made no impression. He could not be heard. A few years later electric recording turned him into a star, with a pleasing and melodious soft lights manner. His "Blue Skies" is a delight. But Vickie took her stand by virtue of her playing skill in halls unwired for sound and to which she brought a touch of showmanship and style, a glance of approval from her fellows, perhaps even from the bass fiddler. Her self-assurance and sense of style stayed with her to the end. There was a professional freemasonry to the Business. Entrance to it and acceptance was jealously guarded. Vickie Cornettie was evidently part of it, a merited distinction.

A typical Variety dressing-room

She is unknown now. But it is a pleasure to recall her and, through her pay tribute to those many like her who got an act together and worked it up to the level of an art so that her name was always a pleasure to read on the booking sheets.

Peter Fannan, Vickie Cornettie – indeed all those who are mentioned in these pages deserve a note of recognition. Talented, original, frail, human: as various as Life itself. Insignificant, perhaps in these days of publicity mechanisms and Mass Media.

But real, alive, vital, so that despite the changes in style, appeal, fashion and in Society itself, they demand much more than a passing footnote.

Their existence was a central part of real Theatre. New and Forthcoming Attractions must not obscure the central part Variety played in the Entertainment Life of the Nation.

"Cruikshank" in 1918

ENSA EXPERIENCES OF DAVE & JOE O'GORMAN

What did you do in the War, Dad?

The answer to this query, for children of variety artistes, was frequently, "I entertained the troops." And it was certainly the case for me for Dad and Uncle Dave, the O'Gorman Brothers were well-known on the circuit of troop entertainment. Having worked extensively throughout the U.K. (touring the shows that they had appeared in, "Magic Carpet" at the Prince's Theatre, W.1., round the larger bases and camps and Depots, such as R. M. Barracks Eastney and giving a show for the Invasion forces confined to the West Ham Stadium) they were finally able to get passages to Italy, by sea, and to India and Burma by air. It was no easy matter to obtain transport, such was the pressure on space and aircraft and this was a point often overlooked by those who criticised artistes for not making themselves available.

So it was that in the early Autumn of 1944, orders were received to report to Liverpool to take ship to Italy. Security was very strict. It was impossible to telephone from the dock area or indeed to communicate in any way. However, the Company was soon aboard the "Queen of Bermuda," formerly a luxury cruise liner, now involved in a different sort of cruising and at dawn set off down the Irish Sea, one of the great convoy of ships bound apparently for the Mediterranean. It was a shock to find one morning that no other vessels were in sight, the other ships having turned off during the night for America. Despite the confidence of the crew that the liner could out-run any U-Boat, it was more than relief to make port in Naples safely.

ENSA matters were organised in Naples by Major Neville Willing, who later became manager of the Café de Paris and he was very helpful in making all the arrangements.

Dave and Joe had a very good company with them: Dot Doreen, the Radio Three close harmony singers, Nicola Sterne, Edith Haley, Alice Stevenson, Gwendo Paull and George Robertson. Dot Doreen, a niece of Florrie Forde, was a very great asset. She had an attractive bell-like voice and was a good tapper. By this time she had already done a good deal of work for ENSA.

The first show was at an American hospital in Naples. Here one G.I. was heard to remark, "Say this is better than the Bob Hope Show!" which if not strictly true, was at least an indication that things were on the right lines. Certainly the Americans showed their appreciation in fine style: flowers and chocolates for the girls and boxes of cigars for Dave O'Gorman (Joe did not smoke) and for George Robertson.

Naples was inclined to be a bit dangerous at night so the Company was very pleased to find the transport arrangements in the capable hands of Alec and Eric Bedser, who were in the RAF Police section. They laid on a comfortable saloon car for which the Company was very grateful. Another good friend from the Surrey cricket scene was Eddie Watts whom Dave and Joe met at Cesena. He was serving in the RASC.

Monte Cassino, Italy, 1944

Moving to Rome, by way of Cassino, where the devastation was frightful, gave the members of the company sober reminders of the reality of this war zone. Regularly notices would appear, "Keep to taped areas marked CLEAR" and "Warning! Danger of MINES. Death is permanent."

In Rome the Company appeared at the Argentine Theatre together with Semprini. Here all arrangements in the hands of Major Nigel Patrick. The Company also had the privilege of a small audience with His Holiness, Pope Pius XII. His blessing, "To you and your family" was an abiding memory and source of strength later on.

Leaving Rome the party got on with its real business of entertaining troops near the front line, visiting on both sides of the Appenines the 5th and 8th Armies. Their route took them through Florence, Livorno, Perugia, Ancona, Cesena and Forli and hard up behind the Front Line. Twice the convoy was split up, with vehicles 100 yards apart as the road came under fire. (Joe's son, then serving as pilot in the RAF was highly indignant when he heard later that this had been allowed to happen to non-combatants well over military age). At the time Dave and Joe reckoned it was just part of the job.

Weather conditions were appalling, driving rain and fierce winds. The billets provided were fairly primitive and often one oil stove had to be used for heating both the billets and the back stage area. The girls were luckiest, being recipients of fur lined jackets and boots. These were especially handy for trips in Bedford trucks and to don after the shows when wet white had to be washed off in ice-cold water!

One night at Forli, all were awakened in the early hours by the roar of tanks passing by. Fearing a Panzer attack the Company, was soon dressed and ready to make a quick getaway. Relief was profound when it was made known that the sound was of Allied tanks moving North for a renewed offensive against the German forces. In this midst of this the conditions of the local population were hard in the extreme and individuals were pathetically grateful for any surplus rations or supplies. As for cigarettes – well.

In spite of everything the show continued to go on. This letter, received from one who saw the show several times, testifies to the impact made by Joe and Dave.

"They even turned up at Fano on the Adriatic in 1944. It was freezing. Yet they did fifteen shows that we knew about, in the same place, a smallish bombed fruit warehouse on the estuary of a little river. We were all muffled up in RAF greatcoats and anything we could find. They just strolled on as if it were at the London Palladium. Their gags tore the place apart!"

Eventually these European adventures came to an end and the boys boarded the flight home in time for the Pantomime at Coventry. However at the end of the run they were off again, this time further afield, to India and Burma!

1945 India and Burma

Going to the Far East meant having the full programme of inoculations. The Medics suggested a sensible period of rest after them and abstinence from alcohol. Disregarding their advice, one performer decided to have his usual brandy. The price paid was immediate, though temporary collapse. Those jabs certainly packed a punch.

Finally news came that a flight had been arranged and the party assembled at Victoria Station. Nobody knew where the train was to take them and the sense of mystery was increased as they were ushered to a part of the station that nobody in the group had ever visited before – a platform far away from the main concourse. There waiting for them was a luxury train, used it seems for visiting Royalty and Heads of State. The opulence of its fittings was staggering and the Troupe was delighted to realise that its artistes were all V.I.Ps!

The train pulled out and proceeded in a leisurely fashion through the darkened landscape. Even the most experienced travellers had no idea of the route or destination and glances through the Blackout Blinds yielded little information of their whereabouts. Eventually, after some hours the train stopped and the word came to alight.

There was a sea tang to the air. With faltering steps the groups found themselves being ushered into a motor boat which set off quickly into the darkness. Soon a huge black shape filled the sky which was gradually identified as a Sunderland Flying Boat. This was their transport to India.

ENSA Company, India, 1945

Their mysterious Midnight journey had taken them to Poole Harbour.

The first stop was Augusta where they rested overnight. Then on again to Cairo. However, engine trouble occurred as they were crossing the Mediterranean and a forced landing had to be made. This caused great consternation to the two MPs who shared the flight and were anxious to get on, to Chungking. All remonstrations were firmly dealt with by the Brigadier, who was OC Flight. Also on board was a mysterious Mr. Ryan who disappeared at Cairo.

Though his name was repeatedly called at all subsequent stops, nothing more was heard of him.

During the stay at Cairo the party was entertained by Whip Wheatley, the jockey who was training in Egypt. It seemed strange that such activities should be in full swing with the war still raging.

Flying on by way of the Habaniyeh and Bahrein, they finally made landfall at Karachi. Here they were met by Toby Welch, a cricketer and fellow entertainer, whom Joe had last seen at Bradford hitting the famous bowler, Verity for 24 in one over! Wasting little time, they moved quickly to Delhi where the company was brought up to strength with the arrival of a soprano and a soubrette. With them was a liaison man, Sgt. Jock Walker. Jock was charming and efficient and was soon on very friendly terms with Dave and Joe. He brought with him a Gurkha, Bahadur Sing, who had been invalided from the Calvert Column of Chindits. He too was to be a tower of strength, for he knew how to make tents and basha huts and to render these as comfortable living places.

The real business soon started with a Broadcast from Delhi and a show at the Irwin Stadium. This was followed by a series of moves by train taking in Roorkee and Dehra Dun ("Watch your saluting!") Saharampur and Gwalior, which took a long time. The train went so slowly that it was possible to sit on the step of the compartment to keep cool and take a little sun. At Gwalior they saw the fort captured by British soldiers in the 19th century. The effort needed to do so, climbing the heights under the blazing sun wearing heavy uniforms, was unimaginable.

It was at Saharampur that the Company's soubrette Frances James was taken ill and the C.O.'s wife nursed her, missing the show in the process; she had not seen a show of any sort for years. The soubrette had, of course, to accompany the Troupe on the train. The young lady was brought to the station in an ambulance and placed on a stretcher. But the station was crammed with Hindus going on a pilgrimage and when the train drew in it was soon filled to capacity, with dozens more hanging on to the outside. Many of the pilgrims were handicapped and some were carrying beds of nails. The whole party had to stand around the invalid to protect her and to make sure she had a supply of air. Through the kindness of a Catholic priest who was taking a party of school boys to the hills for the hot weather a compartment was made available to give her space and as much fresh air as possible.

Lady Artistes. At Roorkee the troops requested that the Ladies wear some pretty dresses and they were glad to oblige. However, the Adjutant made a request in his turn that Uniform should be warn at all times apart from stage performances as all personnel were under Army control.

On the other hand when due to give a show on a warship the message came that boys would like to see the girls as they should be dressed. On the return to shore in a landing craft Eileen Murphy stood at the front and was drenched by the spray. This plus the effect of the hot sun caused her dress to shrink visibly up beyond her waist!

All suffered from upset stomachs, some from sunburn and prickly heat. The compulsory mepachrine turned everybody yellow and the compulsory intake of salt was a daily ordeal, for George Robertson especially.

So by way of Dillawari – where the main amusement at other times was shooting on the range which had caused, it was said, the expenditure of more ammunition than in the whole of the Burma Campaign so far – to Calcutta, where the request was made, "Will you go to Burma?" Of course that was why they were there.

So the very next morning the whole party, baggage and mini piano were loaded with a full load of other stores on a Dakota with orders for Akyab. The weather was a bit uncertain in the Pre-Monsoon period and clouds were gathering as they took off in the heavily laden plane. Ad after about half an hour's flying the weather closed in and they were flying through a fully fledged thunderstorm. The rain beat on the wings and the plane pitched and bucked in the wind. Suddenly the plane was flipped over on its back and began to fall upside down and quite out of control. Eventually the down draught ceased and, with its engines howling, the pilot regained level flight. He had to do this gradually as most people were thrown to end up lying on the roof of the cabin. All the people except Joe, who, looking to make himself comfortable, had made a bed on top of some soft kit bags, stacked up on one side of the plane. He had secured himself by loops, normally used to hold the cargo in place.

During the awful downward plunge he had been suspended from the roof! Gradually, order was restored. It was remarkable that the piano had not broken loose. The violence of the tropics having spent itself the pilot was able to offer a few words. "That was the most incredible experience of my flying career. I had no control at all. We will never be closer to Death than that until our time comes."

This episode shows the courage it took to fly under Monsoon conditions in the Burma Campaign, a crucial factor in the supply of the ground troops and the eventual defeat of the Japanese.

Landing craft at the recapture of Rangoon, 1945

With their orders, for Akyab the plane eventually touched down at a desolate airstrip. The heat compounded by the metal runway was terrific. As the party disembarked the pilot said, "I'll get you some transport." "Will that take us to Akyab?" "Akyab? This is Ramree. My orders were to drop you here." Consternation all round but having been shown the orders he agreed to take them back to Akyab. Having eventually landed there – there were many others with priority – they were greeted by Major Davidson, a cricketing companion from the Richmond Club. "What are you doing here?" "We're here to do some entertaining." "Not here – Akyab!" So after a rest they boarded again and reached Ramree. Not a soul in sight. They rested under the wings in the scorching heat after a while a lone figure approached. His suggestion that Akyab was their true destination was greeted with some disapproval!

A long trek to the Command post produced a truck and a warm welcome to the RAF billets.

During the night, a signal came from General Leese that a special show was to be given for the Lincolnshire Regiment who had had a tough time.

The journey entailed a very long difficult journey in four-wheel drive trucks and again on arrival nobody knew anything about it!

However, the chance for Entertainment was not to be wasted and a stage was mocked up and in the approved style with the troops camouflaged and surrounded by slit trenches nursing their weapons and the light provided by the headlamps of trucks the show was duly given.

The soubrette, Frances James, managed her tapdance on the zinc laid on the sand and every joke and song went over big. But the highlight was the soprano singing, "Just a song at Twilight" and to hear the chorus of men's voices ringing out through the still night air was an incredibly moving experience. The troupe felt that the whole enterprise was worthwhile.

By the time of their return Joe's catch phrase, "I think I'll walk about" was known throughout the Sub-Continent. So much so that in a cinema in Calcutta, right in the middle of a very dull film one soldier and got up and said loudly, "Well I think I'll walk about!" and the resultant roar lasted for about two minutes.

In all the company did 55 shows the final ones being for the RAF at Jessore. While there Rangoon was recaptured and Peace came to Europe. All this gave a feeling that the job was worthwhile.

However, there were two riders to emphasise that all was not sweetness and light.

Jock Walker received a letter from his father, saying, "Well son you'll be coming home soon back to Glasgow. Make sure you bring your rifle with you!"

And on return to UK, Dave collapsed at the Empire, Liverpool, with delayed Malaria. There were tensions and stresses to be endured.

The Company in India were, Dave and Joe O'Gorman, George Robertson (Impersonator), Lydia Davis (Pianist), Frances James (Soubrette), Eileen Murphy (Comedienne).

- oo0oo -

Conclusion

"Well, it's been nice talking to you. They are coming in for the second house now so I had better get ready. The running order has been changed."

"The Great Carlos! Five minutes please!"

Ladies and Gentlemen. This was Variety.

Acknowledgements

My thanks are due to all those who have helped me with this project. I am greatly indebted to them.

Max Tyler (Historian British Music Hall Society)
Terry Lomas (British Music Hall Research Group)
Dick Playle (British Music Hall Society)
Graeme Cruikshank (Archivist Palace Theatre, London)
Peter Baynham-Honri
Terry Frost (Historian Bradford City AFC)
Nick Charlesworth - Printing and technical advice
Moya Clarkson (Daughter of Peter Fannan)
My wife Kathleen for forbearance over the litter of books and all my family for help and encouragement.

Sources consulted

"The Performer" 1930-1955; "Alexandra Theatre" M. F. K. Fraser; account ledgers for Coventry Hippodrome and New Theatre, Northampton; press cutting books for Holborn Empire; Finsbury Park Empire; Penge Empire; Brighton Hippodrome. Handwritten manuscript of memoirs of Joe O'Gorman (Jnr.)

Index

Numbers in bold refer to illustrations

82